HAIRPIN CROCHET

PAMELA THOMPSON

HAIRPIN
CROCHET
TECHNIQUE AND DESIGN

B.T. Batsford Ltd, London

photographs by Trevor Bray ARPS AMPA
line drawings by Pamela Thompson and
Clifford Thompson

First published 1983

© Pamela Thompson 1983

ISBN 0 7134 3952 1

Filmset by Servis Filmsetting Ltd, Manchester
Printed in Great Britain by
The Anchor Press Ltd, Tiptree, Essex
for the publishers,
B.T. Batsford Ltd,
4 Fitzhardinge Street, London W1H oAH

4

CONTENTS

Acknowledgements 7
Introduction 8
How to use this book
including: conversion charts and
  abbreviations

I HAIRPIN CROCHET BRAIDS 12

1 MATERIALS AND EQUIPMENT 14
  · yarns
  · crochet hooks
  · hairpins

2 WORKING THE BASIC BRAID 16
  · starting hairpin crochet
  · crocheting the basic braid

3 HOW TO USE THE BASIC BRAID 21
  · suggested uses
  · choosing suitable yarns, hooks and
    hairpins
  · working hints
  · how to apply the braid

4 VARIATIONS OF THE BASIC BRAID 27
  (patterns 1–7)

5 DEVELOPING THE BASIC BRAID WITH
  ADDITIONAL CROCHET 30
  · twisting the loops
  · headings and insertions
  (patterns 8–15)

  · working into groups of loops
  · adding further rows of crochet
  · working a corner
  · working a curve
  · suggested uses for decorative braids
  · working a frill
  · working a fringe

II HAIRPIN CROCHET FABRICS 47

6 JOINING THE BRAIDS TOGETHER 48
  · joins using extra yarn
  (patterns 1–7)
  · cable joins
  · decorative braids using joins
  · joining corners
  · working hints for fabrics
  · suggested uses for hairpin fabrics

7 HAIRPIN FAN BRAIDS AND FABRICS 59
  · working fan braids and joins
  · suggested uses for hairpin fans

8 HAIRPIN CROCHET ROUNDS 64
  · a simple round motif
  · edging a round motif
  · ideas for appliqué motifs

9 FABRICS MADE FROM ROUNDS 68
  · joining wheel motifs

· a mohair Armenian shawl
· enlarging the basic motif
· ideas for doilies
· old hairpin doilies

10 MAKING A TRIANGULAR SHAPE *82*
· shawl
· variations using the triangular shape

III CREATIVE HAIRPIN
CROCHET *85*

11 COMBINING TECHNIQUES *86*
· combining different widths of braid
· combining braid and ribbon
· combining joins
· combining textures

12 BRAID LACES *95*
· appliqué braid lace
· Renaissance braid lace
· crochet braid lace

13 HOW TO CREATE AND EXPERIMENT *101*
· preparations
· starting a design

14 HAIRPIN EDGINGS USING A DIFFERENT
TECHNIQUE *104*
(patterns 1–7)
· working the edging
· variations

15 HISTORICAL NOTES *111*
· the development of hairpin crochet
· old tools
· old braids

Bibliography *117*
List of Suppliers *118*
Index *119*

ACKNOWLEDGEMENTS

The author wishes to thank all the people who gave help, encouragement and information. To the Trustees of the Rachel B. Kay Shuttleworth Collections, Gawthorpe Hall, Burnley, Lancashire for their permission to photograph figures 48, 49 and 71, Dr J. Widdowson of Sheffield University, Mrs J. Osler, Miss Wood, Mrs B. Roebuck, and all the many correspondents for their patterns and reminiscences. To my photographer Trevor Bray, ARPS, AMPA, also my husband Clifford Thompson for figures 48, 49 and 71 and to my mother-in-law who first taught me how to use a hairpin.

INTRODUCTION

Hairpin crochet is an old craft, its origins being obscure and mainly a matter of guesswork. There is, however, proof that this branch of crochet work was very popular well over a hundred years ago when Victorian ladies created crochet lace of beautiful delicacy using a crochet hook and their long hairpins. Modern hairpin work takes advantage of the great variety of yarns now available, and many effects can be achieved from dainty edgings to lovely, crunchy, wool textures.

The basic piece of hairpin crochet is a simple braid crocheted round a hairpin-shaped tool using a normal crochet hook, its chief quality being the light lacy loops formed on each side. After overcoming the initial difficulty of holding an extra tool, hairpin crochet is found to be a fairly simple craft bringing swift results and an economical use of yarn. The resulting basic braid is then ready to use as an edging or for decorative borders and can be further developed by varying the crochet stitches and adding more crochet embellishments. Unique hairpin fabrics can also be made by joining several strips together, a pleasure to make and a delight to look at.

Most of the braid patterns in this book have been collected from older ladies who learnt this particular skill from their mothers, aunts or grandmothers. Some of them had never used a printed pattern and during my research in museums, old books and periodicals I have not found any written evidence of some of the examples these ladies so kindly sent me.

From the knowledge passed down to us it is possible to adapt many of these patterns to suit our modern needs using a wider range of yarns than the needleworker has ever known. The designs in this book are mostly modern and practical, but a few are unashamedly Victorian – my tribute to our industrious and painstaking forebears.

HOW TO USE THIS BOOK

LEARN TO CROCHET FIRST

Hairpin crochet is one branch of several crochet-based crafts and it is therefore necessary to have some experience of basic crochet prior to starting hairpin work. Some of the applications in this book require a working knowledge of only the simplest crochet stitches – these are chain, double crochet (single crochet) and treble (double crochet) – but to avoid frustration it is advisable to attain proficiency in handling the hook and yarn to produce an even tension before taking up the hairpin.

HOW THE CONTENTS ARE PRESENTED

The contents of this book have been set out in three parts, the first of which deals with the working of the basic braid and its variations and further development by adding additional crochet to give even more lacy appeal. The second part shows how the braids may be joined together to form very attractive fabrics whilst the third part gives suggestions and instructions for particular items.

THE STUDY SCHEME

In order to use this book to the full and to avoid disappointments it is suggested that the student starts at the beginning and works through each stage in Parts I and II. This not only ensures a complete understanding of this craft, but it will

also prove to make it easier to work the instructions in Part III, as certain techniques will be explained as they arise. By working small samples at each stage the worker will soon achieve a relaxed, rhythmic action, produce an even tension and also become aware of the possibilities and limitations of this form of crochet work. It would be unrealistic to insist that all the items in Part III should be made up. These patterns have been supplied to illustrate how techniques can be combined and adapted. It will be sufficient to read the introductions and study the illustrations.

PRACTISING HAIRPIN CROCHET

Hairpin crochet is quickly worked and even more quickly pulled back, so there is little tedium in practising and experimenting. It is also very adaptable and the worker will soon see that it is easy to 'invent' variations. There would not be enough room in one book to show all the possibilities; those that have been included are judged to be suitable for the purpose, of design that is pleasing and not contrived for its own sake.

USING THE ILLUSTRATIONS

The photographs are numbered consecutively and called 'figure 1' etc. In the later stages of the book there are a few references to earlier techniques so by quoting either the figure or diagram number they should be easy to find. Before taking up the hairpin and crochet hook, study the relevant illustrations to form a rough idea of the processes involved. When working through the instructions refer to the illustrations constantly.

CONVERSION CHARTS

This book caters for British and American readers, but as tool sizes and terms are different and measurements are being converted to the metric system it is possible that some confusion may occur. These tables are set out for easy reference should the worker need guidance, especially when doing freelance work.

Hooks and yarns
Since 1969 British crochet hooks have been manufactured to the new international (metric) range. Many people will still have hooks made to the old British standards and these will probably be in circulation for many years yet. This is further complicated by the fact that American hook sizes and terms differ from the British.

This table shows the old British, the new metric and the American equivalents. The fourth column gives a rough estimate of the type of yarn suitable for the hook size. The wool-type yarns are described in very basic terms which are intended to convey the thickness. Manufacturers are producing so many different types it is advisable to check the yarn with the hook.

Several sizes do not convert exactly, so some columns show two options.

Old British	International (metric)	American	Suggested yarn type for Hairpin Crochet
Steel 6	0.06 mm	Steel 14	Mercer crochet 80/70
Steel 5	0.075 mm	Steel 12	Mercer crochet 60
Steel 4	1.00 mm	Steel 9 or 10	Mercer crochet 40/30
Steel 3	1.25 mm	Steel 8 or 9	Mercer crochet 20
Steel $2\frac{1}{2}$	1.50 mm	Steel 7	M.C. 10 (Knit-Cro-Sheen)
Steel 2	1.75 mm	Steel 6	Perle cotton 8
Steel 1 Aluminium 14	2.00 mm	B1	Perle cotton 5
Steel 2/0 Aluminium 12	2.50 mm	C2	Knitting cotton
Aluminium 11	3.00 mm	D3	3-ply
Aluminium 9	3.50 mm	E4, F5	4-ply craft cotton
Aluminium 8	4.00 mm	G6	Double knitting
Aluminium 7	4.50 mm	7 or 8	Double knitting
Aluminium 6	5.00 mm	H8	Aran
Aluminium 5	5.50 mm	I9 or J10	Chunky
Aluminium 4	6.00 mm	J10	Mohair
Aluminium 2	7.00 mm	K$10\frac{1}{2}$	Rug wool

The working instructions in this book give the metric crochet-hook sizes with the American sizes in brackets, e.g. 1.50 mm (Steel 7)

Hairpin widths

These are also being converted from the old Imperial measurements to the metric sizes shown below. It will be noticed that the metric hairpin widths offer a wider range than the old sizes and in some cases are only approximate equivalents. The instructions quote the metric width with inches in brackets, e.g. 35 mm ($1\frac{1}{2}$ in).

10 mm	$-\frac{1}{2}$ in	45 mm	$-1\frac{3}{4}$ in
15 mm	$-\frac{1}{2}$ in	50 mm	-2 in
20 mm	$-\frac{3}{4}$ in	60 mm	$-2\frac{1}{2}$ in
25 mm	-1 in	70 mm	$-2\frac{3}{4}$ in
30 mm	$-1\frac{1}{4}$ in	80 mm	-3 in
35 mm	$-1\frac{1}{2}$ in	100 mm	-4 in
40 mm	$-1\frac{1}{2}$ in		

Metric measurements of length

The measurements used in this book are given in metric terms with Imperial conversion in the brackets, e.g. 2.5 cm (1 in).

STITCH CONVERSIONS AND ABBREVIATIONS

This chart shows the British crochet-stitch terms set beside the American equivalents. The brackets hold the abbreviated terms which are used in the pattern instructions. The British version is given first with the American stitch in brackets, e.g. 2 dc (sc).

British	American
slip stitch (sl st)	slip stitch (sl st)
chain (ch)	chain (ch)
double crochet (dc)	single crochet (sc)
half treble (htr)	half double crochet (hdc)
treble (tr)	double crochet (dc)
double treble (dtr)	treble (tr)

loop (s) lp (s)   group (s) grp (s)

Glossary of hairpin terms

loops – the outer loops of hairpin braid

group – a number of loops taken up together with one crochet stitch

spine – the central crochet of a hairpin braid

foundation braid – completed braid ready for additional crochet or for joining

These terms are all explained the first time they come up in the text and are given here for easy reference.

I

HAIRPIN CROCHET BRAIDS

MATERIALS AND EQUIPMENT

YARNS

The choice of yarn depends entirely on its suitability for the work being planned and as in normal crochet work this can range from fine cottons to bulky wools. The nature of hairpin work makes it possible to experiment quickly and economically with the more unusual yarns, including novelty, metallic, string and raffia type once the basic patterns have been mastered.

CROCHET HOOKS

The hook is chosen to match the yarn being used, that is, a fine hook for fine cottons, a larger hook for wools, to give good, even tension which allows the yarn to be held easily in the hook and pass smoothly through the stitch.

HAIRPINS

Hairpins, sometimes called forks or staples, can be purchased in a variety of widths, the smallest being 10 mm ($\frac{1}{2}$ in) the largest 100 mm (4 in). In the past ladies used their own hairpins, but most modern hairdressing pins are too flimsy. Pins may be available through local stockists of knitting and crochet supplies. Alternatively they can be made at home from old metal knitting pins bent to shape after heating, and

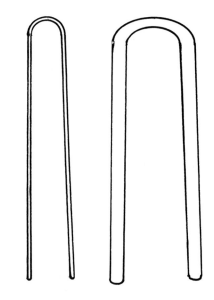

Diag 1a Actual size fine pin
Diag 1b Some pins have slightly splayed prongs

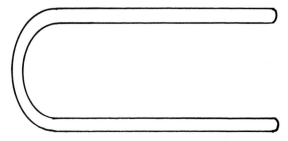

Diag 1c Wider pins have thicker prongs. Correct length approx. 13 cm (5 in)

these should be rigid with smooth tips (diagrams 1a, 1b, 1c).

AN IMPROVISED HAIRPIN (DIAGRAM 2)

This hairpin can be made quickly and relatively cheaply by using short double-pointed knitting pins or two cable pins. These are pushed firmly into two bottle corks, taking care that they are equidistant. This will result in a longer pin which will therefore hold more loops. If aluminium pins are used this tool is quite light. When the pin is full, remove the cork from one end and slip off most of the loops, replace the cork and continue.

HAIRPIN LOOM OR QUAD FRAME (DIAGRAM 3)

The experienced worker who wishes to make a variety of larger articles will find this tool a valuable aid to be used instead of the bent hairpin. The main advantages are that it holds a large number of loops, is adjustable to several widths between 50 mm (2 in) and 100 mm (4 in) and being made of alloy and plastic is very light in use. It is possible to make a similar frame using a pair of 4.50 mm (7) knitting needles and two 12 cm ($4\frac{3}{4}$ in) lengths of 12.5 mm ($\frac{1}{2}$ in) square wood drilled as shown with a 4.50 mm ($\frac{3}{16}$ in) drill.

The correct width of the pin will depend on the desired result. Fine cotton yarn used with a narrow pin provides a dainty edging, wool used with the same narrow pin results in an attractive braid. Wider pins produce more openwork results.

The beginner is advised to use a 20 mm ($\frac{3}{4}$ in) pin, a 4.00 mm (G6) crochet hook and double knitting wool.

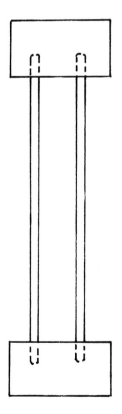

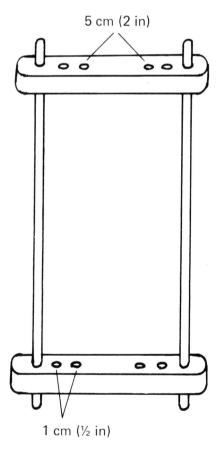

5 cm (2 in)

1 cm (½ in)

Diag 2 An improvised hairpin

Diag 3 Hairpin loom or quadframe

2
WORKING THE BASIC BRAID

STARTING HAIRPIN CROCHET

In order to start crocheting a hairpin braid it is necessary to 'cast on' so that there is a loop around each prong of the hairpin with a stitch on the hook in the centre, as illustrated in diagram 9. This is achieved by following the instructions:

1 Make a slip loop as shown (diagrams 4a, 4b).

2 Slip it over both prongs of the hairpin, adjusting the loop to fit firmly and having the knot at the centre back (diagram 5).

3 Take the hairpin, open end down, between the thumb and forefinger of the left hand (left-handed workers please reverse instructions). Hold the hook and the long end of the yarn in the normal crocheting position, the short end held firmly with the thumb (diagram 6).

4 Pass the hook underneath the loop round the prongs and catch the yarn (diagram 7).

5 Draw the hook to the front and pass it over the loop round the prongs. Catch the yarn and work 1 ch (diagram 8).

    The casting on is now complete (diagram 9).

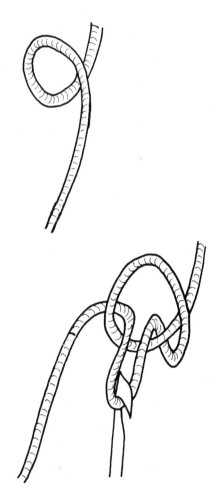

Diag 4a, 4b Making a slip loop

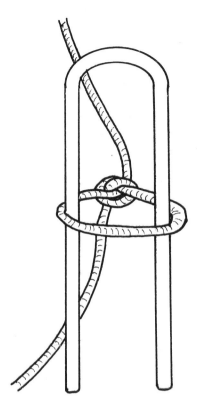

Diag 5 Positioning the slip loop on the hairpin

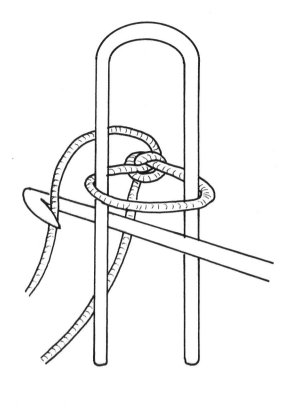

Diag 7 & **8** Stages for casting on

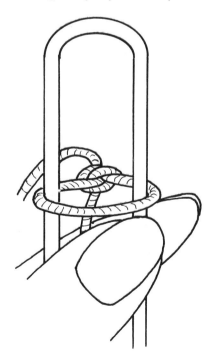

Diag 6 Holding the hairpin

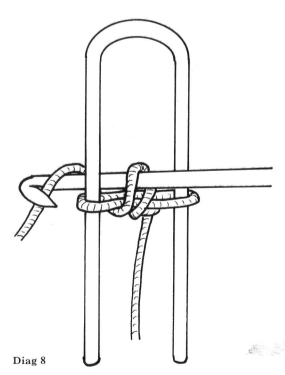

Diag 8

CROCHETING THE BASIC BRAID

The crochet work at the centre of the braid is very simple, consisting of 1 dc (sc) and 1 ch. The loops are formed round the prongs by turning the pin over after each row (figure 1).

Cast on as explained.

1 Work 1 dc (sc) into the front of the left lp, i.e. insert the hook under the front of the left lp (diagram 10) yarn over hook and draw through (2 lps on hook) yarn over hook and draw through the 2 lps on the hook. 1 dc (sc) now completed.

2 Remove the hook from the stitch and turn the hairpin over, bringing the right prong forward from right to left (diagram 11). The yarn is now wrapped round the right prong.

3 Insert the hook back into the stitch and catch the yarn to work 1 ch (diagram 12).

Repeat stages 1, 2 and 3 for the desired length, finishing with the dc (sc). It can easily be remembered as '1 ch, 1 dc (sc), turn'. Fasten off in the usual manner by cutting the yarn and drawing it through the loop on the hook.

Diag 9 The completed stitch

Fig 1 The basic braid

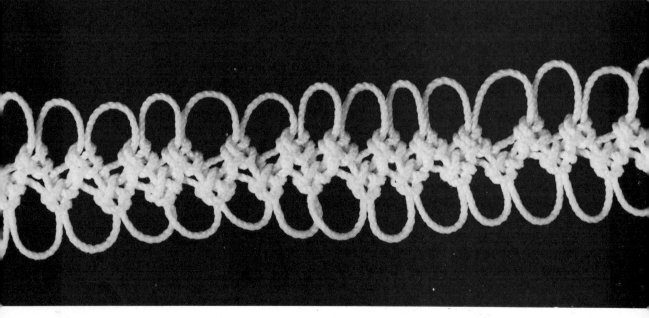

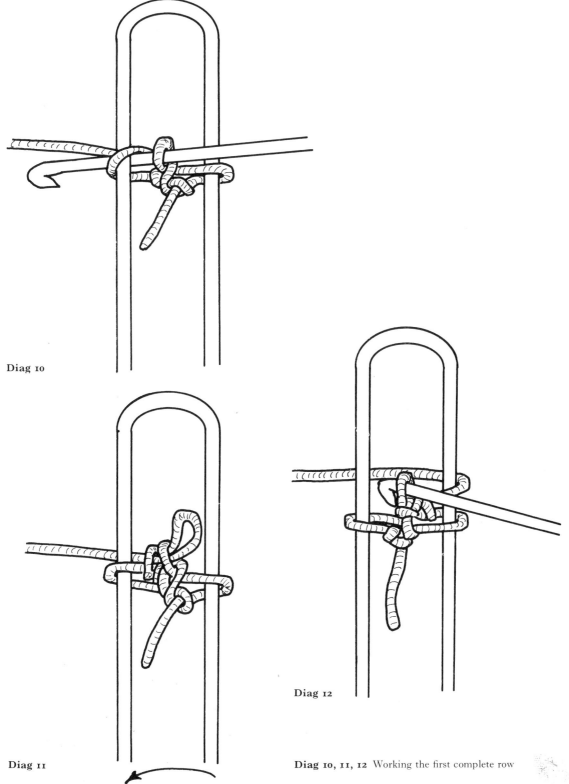

Diag 10

Diag 11

Diag 12

Diag 10, 11, 12 Working the first complete row

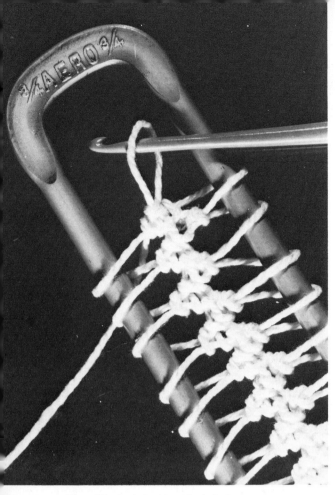

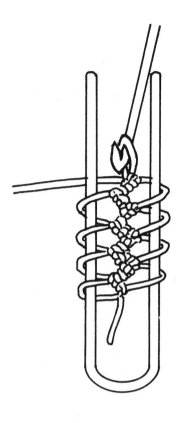

Fig 2 The basic braid on the hairpin

Diag 13 An alternate method of holding the hairpin

Figure 2. Work in progress showing the loops around the prongs. The double crochet has just been worked into the front left loop and the pin is now ready for turning.

AN ALTERNATIVE METHOD

At the first attempts, taking the hook out of the stitch before turning the pin may seem tedious, but practice soon overcomes any clumsiness. However, the braid can be worked with the hairpin being held with the open end up-permost. In this case the hook need not be withdrawn from the stitch in order to turn the prong, but passed between the prongs (diagram 13). When the pin is full the work is then slipped off and the last two pairs of loops are replaced on the prongs to continue working. This must be

done carefully to avoid twisting the braid or the loops. Care must also be taken that the open ends are not drawn together when using this method, as the loops will then be of uneven width. Some hairpins are manufactured with the prongs splayed to allow for this.

3
HOW TO USE THE BASIC BRAID

Having mastered the basic braid it will be found to be a quick and inexpensive way of making an attractive edging for garments and baby blankets, or as a decorative border on clothes or household furnishings. By using a narrow pin and crochet cotton a dainty handkerchief edging can be quickly worked, or it can be used to great effect on small personal items such as book marks, pin cushions, trinket boxes, greeting cards, all reminiscent of those charming Victorian knick-knacks. In fact where a braid or lace is required for practical and decorative purposes hairpin crochet is ideal.

SUGGESTED USES

Diagrams 14a, 14b, 14c. Gay bands stitched on to children's wear such as dungaree bibs, the leg seams of trousers or around skirts.

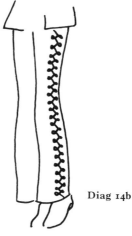

Diag 14b

Diag 14c

Diag 14a, 14b, 14c Using the basic braid on children's wear

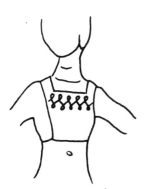

Diag 14a

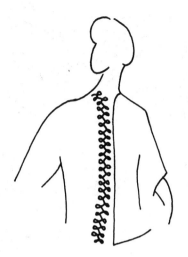

Diag 15 Using a basic braid edging on a Chanel jacket

Diag 17a, 17b Hairpin braid for lampshades and bins

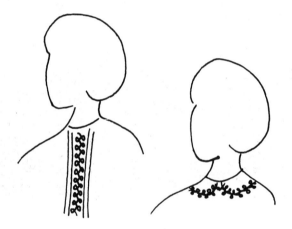

Diag 16a, 16b Finer braids for discreet decoration on clothes

Diagram 15. Used as an edging on a Chanel-type jacket it can be worked in either a toning or a contrasting colour or perhaps a metallic yarn for evening glamour.

Diagrams 16a, 16b. Finer braids add a distinctive touch to dresses and blouses. Perle cotton is ideal for trims on pockets and collars or between rows of pin-stitched tucks.

Diagrams 17a, 17b. Home accessories can also be given edgings of hairpin crochet, e.g. place mats, or it can be used as a braid on lampshades or waste bins.

Having chosen an object for your first venture consult the following hints as to the correct choice of yarns, how to work efficiently and how to apply the finished braid.

CHOOSING SUITABLE YARNS, HOOKS AND HAIRPINS

The choice of yarn is a major factor, as it must be suitable for the project. If the finished article is to be laundered the choice between a natural or synthetic yarn depends on the fibre content of the article on which it is to be used. Natural fibres, especially cotton and wool, may tend to shrink whilst man-made fibres do not. As a general rule avoid using natural fibres on washables unless the label declares shrink resistance.

Figure 3. This photograph shows two braids both of which were worked on a 15 mm ($\frac{1}{2}$ in) hairpin. The upper braid uses a 40 crochet cotton and a 1 mm (Steel 10) crochet hook, the lower braid used a 4 ply yarn with a 3.50 mm (E/4) crochet hook. This gives some indication of the variety of effects possible. The following table is given as a guidance:

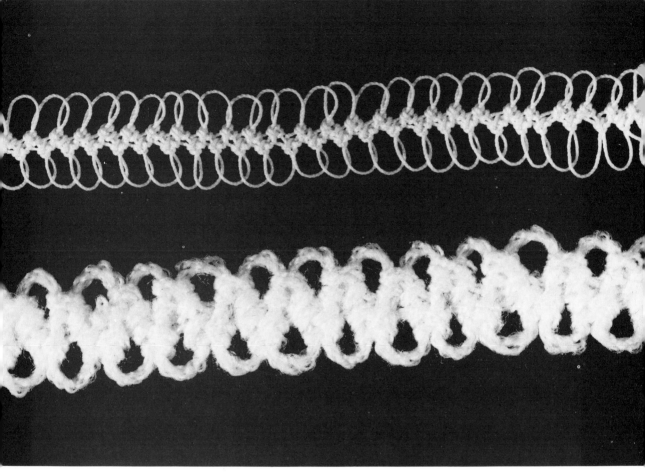

Fig 3 Two lengths of 15 mm (½ in) basic braid using crochet cotton and wool

NARROW LACE EDGINGS SUITABLE FOR
HANDKERCHIEFS

Crochet cotton No. 20 with a 1.25 mm (Steel 9) crochet hook and a 10 mm (½ in) hairpin.
or, for a finer effect:
Crochet cotton No. 40 with a 1.00 mm (Steel 10) crochet hook and 10 mm (½ in) hairpin.

WIDER EDGINGS SUITABLE FOR HOUSEHOLD
LINEN

Crochet cotton No. 10 with a 1.50 mm (Steel 7) crochet hook and a 20 mm (¾ in) or 25 mm (1 in) hairpin.

Fine knitting cotton is also suitable, but may need a larger hook, size 2.00 mm (B1).

DECORATIVE BRAIDS

The width of the hairpin should be chosen according to the desired result. The wider the hairpin the longer the loops. Or consider using two or more narrow braids using different colours.

Double knitting yarn, 4.00 mm (G6) crochet hook and the hairpin width of your choice.

4 ply knitting yarn, 3.50 mm (E4) crochet hook

Perle cotton
This has a pleasing lustrous quality and is available in a wide range of colours. No. 8 and

No. 5 are the most popular, No. 8 being the finer. Nos 3 and 1 are available if a thicker yarn is required. No. 8 perle cotton with 1.50 mm (Steel 7) crochet hook using the narrow hairpin, 10 mm ($\frac{1}{2}$ in) or 20 mm ($\frac{3}{4}$ in). No. 5 perle cotton with a 1.75 mm (Steel 7) crochet hook.

Embroidery threads

These can be used where short lengths of braid are required. Make sure the hank will be long enough, as joins are not recommended. The main advantage is the very wide range of shades available. Use the hook and hairpin sizes suggested for the perle cottons.

Lurex and novelty yarns

This type of yarn is manufactured in great variety. Use any of the previous guides according to the thickness of the yarn being used.

WORKING HINTS

TO PREVENT STRETCHING AND TWISTING

It may be found that when working long lengths the braid has a tendency to twist or stretch. This can be prevented by rolling the braid up as it progresses and securing with an extra length of yarn or a rubber band. A stitch-holder pin as used for knitting is also useful as the loops on one side can be slipped on quickly.

COUNTING THE LOOPS

Should the project require a given number of loops it is useful to mark each 50 loops by tying a short contrasting thread loosely through the loops. The number of loops refers to the number on each side of the braid, e.g. 50 loops on each side.

When finishing off a length of braid it is advisable to leave a fairly long length of yarn, as additional loops can easily be added should these be found to be needed, but for greater efficiency it is better to work more than the number estimated as it is easier to pull extra loops out rather than having to thread loops back on to the hairpin. When the finished length is determined the loose ends may be run in.

STORING WORK IN PROGRESS

To prevent unravelling, draw the stitch on the hook long enough to enable it to be slipped over the end of the hairpin.

ESTIMATING THE REQUIRED LENGTH OF BRAID

Hairpin crochet has an elastic quality which can be exploited. Often the pattern is improved by stretching the braid slightly, but this must not be overdone. After making a rough estimate of the length required, finish off loosely and compare the braid against the article. When the stretch seems right, pin the braid on at each end so that there will be an even distribution of loops. If the braid is to be used round a square article follow the above method for one side only, but do not finish off. When the braid is pinned down count the number of loops used, multiply by 4 and add a further 15 for the corners. This will ensure a uniform distribution on all sides.

HOW TO APPLY THE BRAID

PREPARING THE BRAID

Having worked the correct length of braid, pin it to the article at each end first, then place more pins in between.

HAIRPIN BRAID AS A FULL EDGING (DIAGRAM 18)

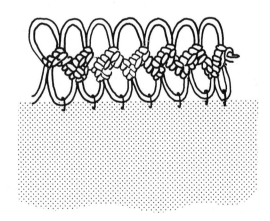

Diag 18 Hairpin braid as a full edging

When using the braid as an edging on hand-kerchiefs, guest towels, collars etc., simply catch each loop along one side of the braid to the edge of the fabric using a small hem stitch and a matching thread.

Turning a corner
To turn a corner neatly lay the fabric item flat and pin together the loops that lie at the corner (possibly three for a narrow braid) and take these up together with a double stitch.

HAIRPIN BRAID AS A HALF EDGING (DIAGRAM 19)

This is more likely to be a wool or decorative yarn braid for use on blankets and garments where the crochet centre of the braid will be stitched along the edge of the item leaving just the outer loops free.

First stitch down the central crochet, using a matching thread and small stitches which should become embedded in the crocheting and therefore almost invisible. In some instances this process may be more satisfactory if done from the back. The inner loops may be left free or caught down.

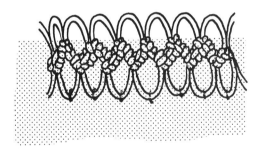

Diag 19 Hairpin braid as a half edging

HAIRPIN BRAID AS A BORDER

Several decorative effects can be obtained when using the braid as a border, and these can give a rich embroidered result by using a variety of yarns and embellishments from the haberdashery shops. The following suggestions are offered as a basis for inspiration.

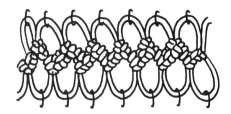

Diag 20 Applying the hairpin braid invisibly

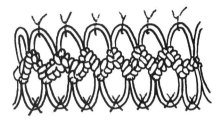

Diag 21 Using additional stitchery

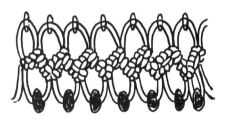

Diag 22 Using beads and sequins with the braids

To apply invisibly (diagram 20)
Catch down the top of each loop with fine matching thread.

Using stitchery as a further decoration
Diagram 21. Catch down the loops with embroidery yarn and a variety of stitches such as a single lazy daisy, a cross stitch etc.
Diagram 22. Catch down with sequins or small beads for a sparkling effect.

Using wide, large, looped braids (diagram 23)
When working with a wider pin and a comparatively finer yarn the braid will appear to be too sloppy, but if couching is used to stitch down the loops the final effect can be quite appealing.

Making shaped borders (diagram 24)
One characteristic of the basic braid is its pliable quality which can easily be exploited to produce

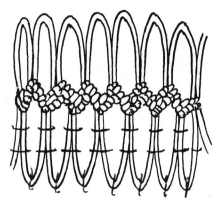

Diag 23 Using couching to stitch down large loops

method especially where the article needs laundering there are instances where it is necessary to use an adhesive. This mainly occurs when using a braid on household articles such as lampshades, waste bins and window blinds.

Using a clear adhesive (such as UHU or Elmer's Glue-all) apply to the central crochet and after marking the exact position stick down carefully, taking care not to stretch the braid too much.

Diag 24 Making shaped borders

curved borders using one or more lengths of braid. Mark the design on to the fabric and stitch down using any of the methods previously explained.

USING ADHESIVE

Although stitching down is by far the better

4
VARIATIONS OF THE
BASIC BRAID

The following braids are a development of the basic method in that the turning of the pin and then catching the yarn with a chain stitch remains constant. The variations occur at the working into the left hand loop, and in the later examples additional chains are also used.

The samples were worked on a 15 mm ($\frac{1}{2}$ in) hairpin using No. 10 crochet cotton and a 1.50 mm (Steel 7) crochet hook (except where stated). The thicker cotton was used for the sake of clarity in the photographs; a finer cotton with a smaller hook will produce a better lacy effect if this is desired. These variations are fun to try and it is advisable to work short lengths of each one to be mounted with adhesive on to a piece of card or paper or even stitched on to a piece of material (a method used by Victorian crochet workers). This will provide the worker with a more superior sampler for future reference than even the best photograph.

For all braids, cast on in the usual manner then work 1 dc (sc) into front LH loop, turn and catch with 1 dc (sc)

BRAID 1 (FIGURE 4)

Work 2 dc (sc) into the front of the left lp. Turn. Catch the yarn with 1 ch. Repeat for desired length. It will be noticed that this produces a wider crochet centre (referred to in future as the spine), and when using a narrow pin the loops will be slightlyshorter. When worked on a wider pin the spine will be more substantial.

Fig 4 Braid 1. Using 2 double crochet (sc)

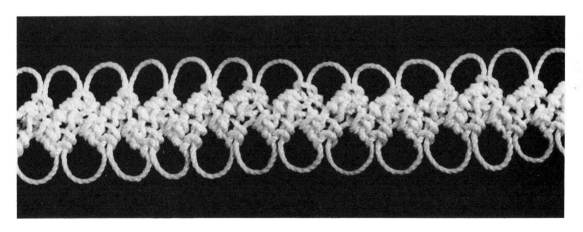

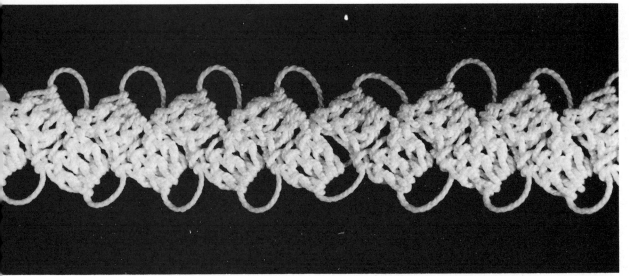

Fig 5 Braid 2. Using 3 trebles (dc)

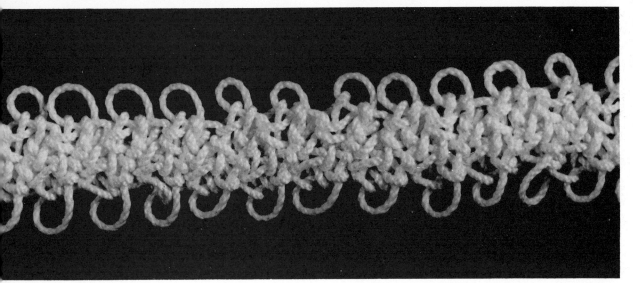

Fig 6 Braid 3. Working into the front and back of the left loop

BRAID 2 (FIGURE 5)

Work 3 tr (dc) into the front of the left lp. Turn. Catch with 1 ch. Repeat.

BRAID 3 (FIGURE 6)

Work 1 dc (sc) into the front of the left lp and 1 dc (sc) into the back of the left lp. Turn. Catch with 1 ch. Repeat.

  This braid is more attractive when worked on a wider pin with a wool-type yarn.

BRAID 4 (FIGURE 7)

Work 1 dc (sc) into the front of the left lp. Turn. Catch with 1 ch and then work 2 more ch (3 ch in all). Repeat.

BRAID 5 (FIGURE 8)

Work 1 tr (dc) 3 ch 1 tr (dc) into the front of the left lp. Turn. Catch with 1 ch. Repeat.

28

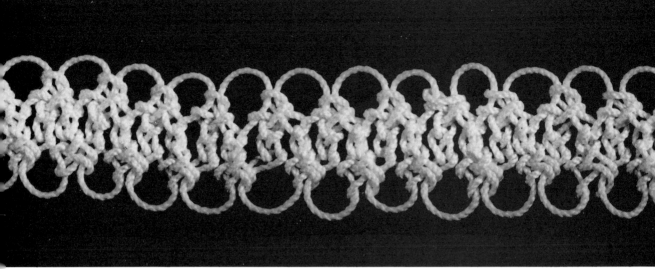

Fig 7 Braid 4. Using 3 chains   Fig 8 Braid 5. Using an extra treble (dc) and chains

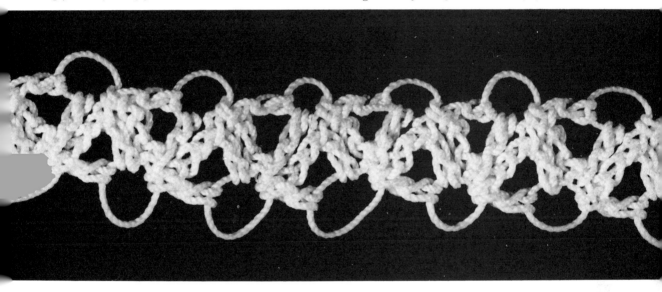

BRAID 6 (FIGURE 9)

Work 2 ch 1 dc (sc) into the front of the left lp. Turn. *Catch with 1 ch 2 dc (sc) under the 1st 2 ch lp (At this stage the first 2 ch lp will not be very distinct). 2 ch 1 dc (sc) into the front of the left lp. Turn. Repeat from *. The 2 ch lps will now be easily seen.

BRAID 7 (FIGURE 10)

Put the hook under the front left lp, draw the thread through. *Pass the thread over the hook and put the hook through the same lp and draw the thread through. Repeat once more from * (6 lps on the hook). Pass the thread over the hook and draw through these 6 lps. Turn. Catch with 1 ch and repeat from the first *.

Many more combinations using double crochet (sc) and trebles (dc) can be worked out, e.g. 1 dc (sc) 1 tr (dc) 1 dc (sc) all into the left lp. Generally the more stitches used in the centre of

29

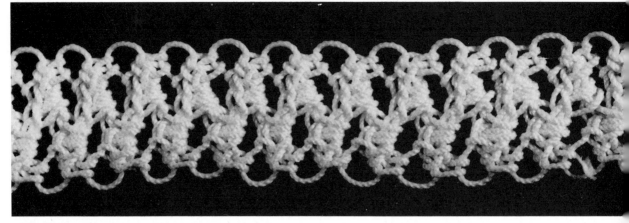

Fig 9 Braid 6. Using extra double crochet (sc) and chains

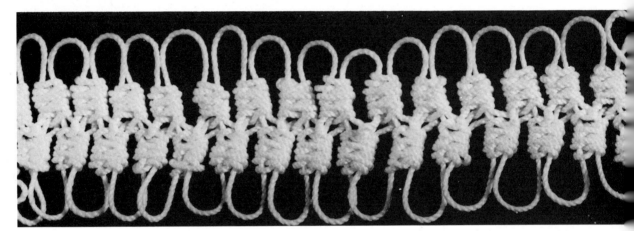

Fig 10 Braid 7. Using a bullion stitch

the braid the more spaced the loops will become.

These braids can be used in any of the ways already suggested. Trying variations with a thicker yarn or a wider pin will often create some surprising results.

5
DEVELOPING THE BASIC BRAID WITH ADDITIONAL CROCHET

The basic braid with all its variations provides a wide selection of edgings and borders. These can be taken a step further by using additional yarn in order to crochet into the loops of a completed length of braid which has been finished off and removed from the hairpin. This is now called the foundation braid.

The following samples were again worked in No. 10 crochet cotton using a 1.50 mm (Steel 7) crochet hook with hairpins of varying widths, the latter being indicated with each example. A contrasting colour has been used so that the additional crochet can easily be recognised. It is not essential to use a yarn of the same thickness as that used for the braid. Often a neater effect is gained by using a finer yarn and a correspondingly smaller hook. The basic braid has been used for the samples, but any of the variations may be used. The additional crochet was worked with No. 20 crochet yarn and a 1.25 mm (Steel 8) hook.

TWISTING THE LOOPS

The worker will now have noticed that often the loops of the braid assume a natural twist so when crocheting into the loops it is important that the loops are either kept flat, or twisted in the same direction, according to the desired effect. The following diagrams show how this is achieved; test with the empty hook first.

AN UNTWISTED OR FLAT LOOP (DIAGRAM 25)

Insert the crochet hook into the front of the loop in readiness to work a double crochet (sc).

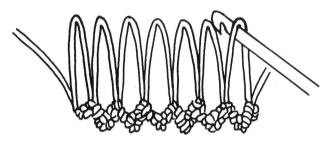

Diag 25 Keeping the hairpin loops flat

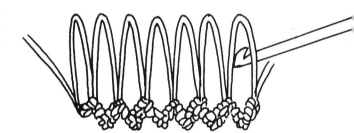

Diag 26 Making a twisted loop

A TWISTED LOOP (DIAGRAM 26)

Insert the crochet hook into the back of the loop; the twist will appear when the double crochet (sc) is worked.

HEADINGS AND INSERTIONS

JOINING IN THE NEW YARN

When using additional yarn make a slip loop on the crochet hook first. Always start the crochet at the casting-on end of the foundation braid to allow for adjustements at the end.

BRAID 8 (FIGURE 11) 15 mm ($\frac{1}{2}$ in) WIDE

Working into the front of each lp work 1 dc (sc) into the 1st lp, 1 ch. Repeat along the length of the braid. Fasten off.

This simple heading can be worked down one side of the braid for an edging with the hairpin loops stitched to the fabric or with the heading stitched to the fabric. When the heading is worked down both sides of the braid a very useful insertion results. Now work another length in the same manner, but twist the loops.

WORKING INTO GROUPS OF LOOPS

In the following sample the loops are twisted in pairs. When two or more loops are taken up together they are now called groups. Try this technique with the empty hook to see how easy and effective this is.

BRAID 9 (FIGURE 12) 15 mm ($\frac{1}{2}$ in) WIDE

Using an even number of loops. Working into the back of each pair, or groups (grp) of 2 lps, 1 dc (sc) into each group, 4 ch. Repeat to the end.

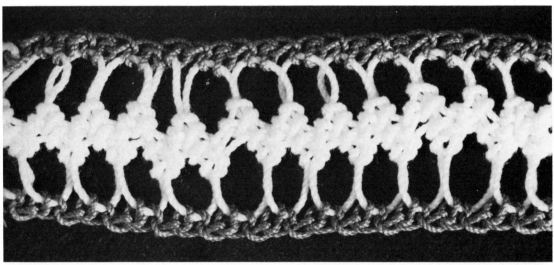

Fig 11 (top) Braid 8. Working a double crochet (sc) into the loops

Fig 12 (bottom) Braid 9. Working a double crochet (sc) into 2 twisted loops

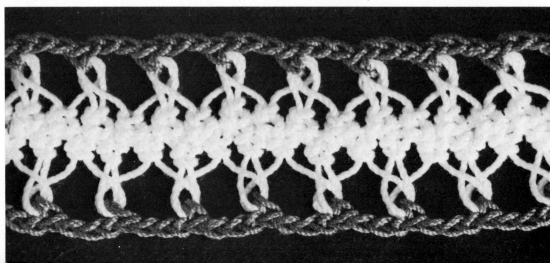

Adjusting the chains

The number of chains worked between the groups must be adjusted according to the yarn being used. It is advisable to work the pattern 4 times, then lay the work down flat to see if any adjustments are necessary. The spine of the braid should be flat and the groups vertical.

BRAID 10 (FIGURE 13) 15 mm ($\frac{1}{2}$ in) WIDE

This example shows how two different headings can be usd on one braid and also includes the use of a picot. The foundation braid has an even number of loops.

Top edge: to work the picot, 1 dc (sc) into the 1st group of 2 twisted lps, 3 ch, 1 sl st into the same dc (sc), 3 ch. Repeat.

Bottom edge: 1 dc (sc) into each untwisted lp, 1 ch. Repeat.

BRAID 11 (FIGURE 14) 20 mm (3/4 in) WIDE

This produces a firm heading with a tiny scalloped effect. The loops are twisted throughout. Use a foundation braid with multiples of 4 loops.

Top edge: work 3 dc (sc) into the 1st grp of 2 lps, 1 ch. Repeat.

Bottom edge: 1 dc (sc) into 1 lp, 1 ch. Repeat.

BRAID 12 (FIGURE 15) 20 mm (3/4 in) WIDE

A group of 4 loops is taken up between blocks of 4 single loops. The loops are twisted throughout. Use a foundation braid with multiples of 4 loops.

Starting with 1 dc (sc) into the 1st lp, work a block of 4 lps with 1 ch between each. 4 ch, 1 dc (sc) into a grp of 4 lps, 4 ch. Repeat from the beginning.

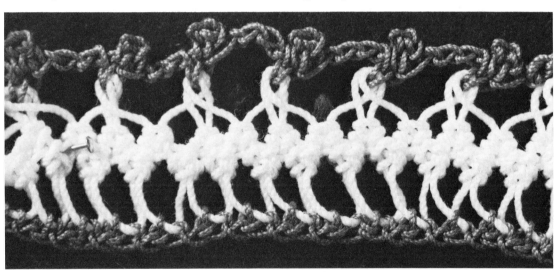

Fig 13 (top) Braid 10. A picot heading   **Fig 14 (bottom)** Braid 11. A tiny scallop heading

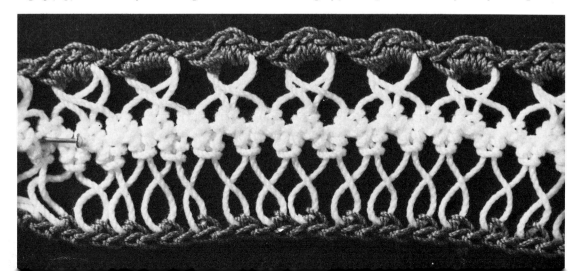

Fig 15 (top) Braid 12. Loops taken up in blocks of 4
single and 4 in a group

Fig 16 (bottom) Braid 13. Crossed loops

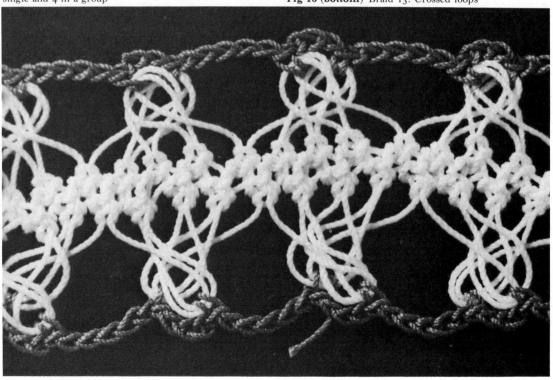

BRAID 13 (FIGURE 16) 25 mm (1 in) WIDE

Crossed loops which are twisted throughout. Use a braid with multiples of 4 loops.

1 dc (sc) into the 1st grp of 2 lps. *5 ch, miss 2 lps, 1 dc (sc) into the next grp of 2 lps, 3 ch, 1 dc (sc) into the 2-lp grp just missed. Repeat from *.

All these samples use groups of 2 loops. Groups of 3 or more can also be used, but a wider foundation braid may be required so that the loops do not drag, especially if a thicker yarn is used. A small experimental sample using 20 loops is recommended.

BRAID 14 (FIGURE 17) 30 mm (1¼ in) WIDE

Making a double twist

Longer loops are required for this dramatic double twist which should be practised with the crochet hook before taking up the extra yarn, as follows:

Fig 17 Braid 14. Double twisted loops

Insert the hook into the back of a 3-lp group as for a normal twist. Swing the blunt end of the hook to the front and continue in this clockwise direction until the full circle is completed and the hook has returned to its normal working position (a double twist completed). Use a foundation braid with multiples of 3 loops.

1 dc (sc) into a double twisted 3-lp group, 5 ch. Repeat.

ADDING FURTHER ROWS OF CROCHET

Further rows of crochet may be added for a bolder effect or where a firm edge is required for practical purposes, especially when used as an insertion. This can be worked in double crochet by working 1 dc (sc) into each dc (sc) and 1 dc (sc) for each ch (working into the ch space as required). If further rows seem desirable care must be taken not to swamp the delicacy of the actual hairpin work with too much or too elaborate extra crochet.

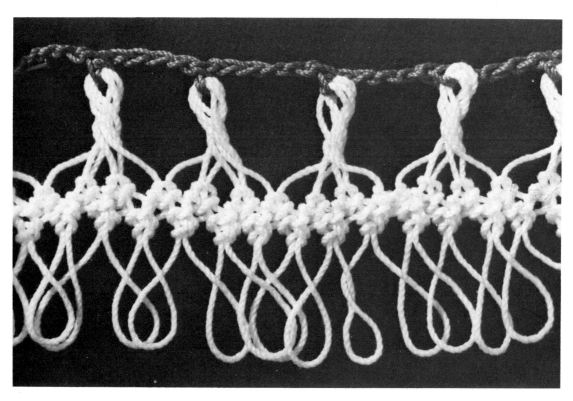

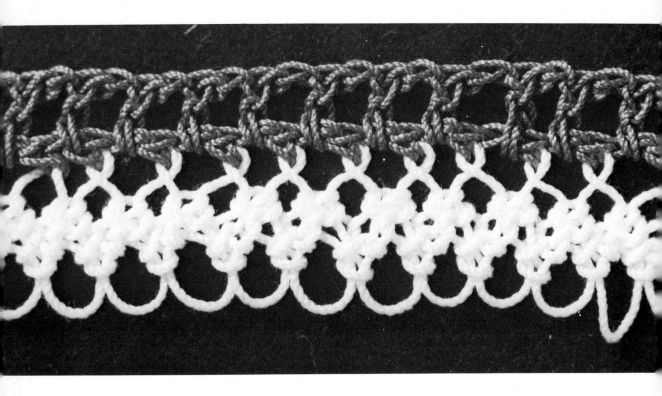

The following braid shows a very useful second row of trebles (double crochets). Where appropriate these could be threaded with a narrow ribbon or a contrasting yarn.

BRAID 15 (FIGURE 18) TREBLE HEADING

1st row: 1 dc (sc) into 1 twisted lp, 1 ch, to the end. 3 ch. Turn.

2nd row: 1 tr (dc) into the first ch space of the previous row, 1 ch, repeat to the end. Fasten off.

The braids already described are just a few of the many permutations which are possible. Varying the twists, the groups and the headings must surely give the worker much pleasure in working out their own versions. When worked in fine yarn these braids give a charming intricate result.

BRAID 16 (FIGURE 19) A FAN EDGING

This very pretty edging illustrates how versatile the headings can be. The crochet on the straight inner edge takes up a large group of 9 loops to

Fig 18 Braid 15. A treble heading (dc)

form a fan effect. The outer edge crochet follows the fan shape to give a curved edge. To show the delicacy of this edging a fine, white, crochet cotton was used for both the braid and headings.

Details
Finished width 20 mm ($\frac{3}{4}$ in). No. 40 crochet cotton. 1.00 mm (Steel 9) crochet hook, 15 mm ($\frac{1}{2}$ in) hairpin.

Braid No. 3 was used for this sample; basic braid is also suitable. Each fan requires 12 loops. A finished fan measures 2.5 cm (1 in). To edge one side of a 22 cm (9 in) handkerchief 108 loops will be needed.

Method
Straight edge. *1 dc (sc) into a grp of 9 lps, 2 ch, (1 dc (sc) into the next lp, 2 ch) 3 times. Repeat from * to the end.

Curved edge *1 dc (sc) 1 ch into each of 8 lps. 1 dc (sc) into the next lp, 1 dc (sc) into a grp of 3 lps. Repeat from * to end.

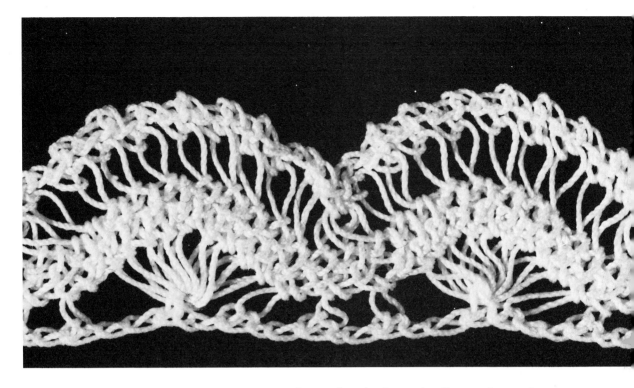

Fig 19 Braid 16. A fan edging

WORKING A CORNER

If a braid with headings is required to fit round a corner a little careful judgement must be used when working the heading. This follows the same principle as used when applying the basic braid to corners as shown in Chapter 3. It is essential to have the article to hand (e.g. a handkerchief) in order to make an approximate calculation of the number of loops required to fit around 4 sides including extra loops for the corners.

METHOD OF WORKING AS SHOWN IN FIGURE 20

1 Work the estimated length of foundation braid and finish off loosely.

2 Work the inner heading using 1 dc (sc), 1 ch, into each loop until it is long enough to fit along one side.

3 Lay this length against the handkerchief, take the braid around the corner and pin

together the loops that lie together at the right angle.

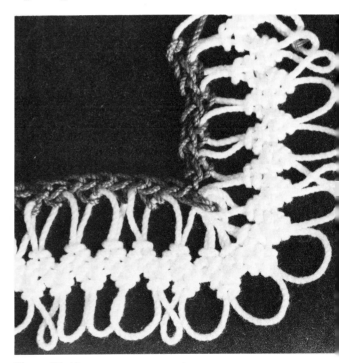

Fig 20 Working a corner

37

4 Take up these loops together with 1 dc (sc).

5 Count the number of loops used for one side and corner and complete the remaining three sides and corners using the same number of loops.

6 Join the heading ends together neatly with 1 sl st. Unpick the loose end of the braid to join the ends of the spine likewise.

7 If an outer edging is to be used, allow extra chains at the corners to ensure the braid lies flat.

For a collar
Use this method to edge a pointed collar, having either the actual garment or a paper pattern to estimate the number of loops needed for 2 short edges, 2 corners and 1 long edge.

The number of loops required at the corners will vary according to the width of the braid and the thickness of the yarn. If the braid is wide and therefore needs a larger number of corner loops these can be taken up in 3 groups to avoid excessive bulk; e.g. to take up 12 loops work 1 dc (sc) into a grp of 4 loops three times (diagram 27). When stitching this type of corner in place attach the middle group exactly on the corner.

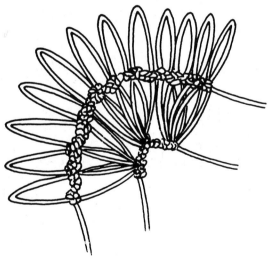

Diag 27 Working a corner

WORKING A CURVE

It will now have been noted that the basic braid and some of the variations possess a pliable quality which enables them to form corners and curves. When further rows of crochet are added this quality is reduced, so when headings are used curves must be built into the extra crochet.

To make a braid with a curved heading the crochet on the inner edge must be adjusted. Usually half as many stitches will be worked into the inner edge as on the outer. Again have the article to hand for checking purposes.

METHOD OF WORKING AS SHOWN IN FIGURE 21

1 Make a sample length of foundation braid with 12 loops.

2 Work the inner edge first: 1 dc (sc) into each lp.

3 Work double the number of crochet stitches on the outer edge as follows: 1 dc (sc), 1 ch into each loop or 2 dc (sc) into each loop.

Checking and adjusting
Lay the worked sample against the desired curve. It is better to do this after working the inner edge. The above instructions will produce an almost circular curve.

If a shallow curve is needed adjust by working 1 dc (sc) into each of 2 loops, 1 ch.

If a tighter circle is needed try 1 dc (sc) into the first lp, 1 dc (sc) into a grp of 2 lps. Continue in this manner working into a single lp and a grp of 2 lps alternately.

Work the outer edge to correspond by adjusting the chains between the loops so that the braid lies flat.

When a satisfactory sample curve is completed it can be used to calculate the approximate number of loops needed for the finished article.

If the braid headings are worked in groups use the same principle, i.e. allow 1 crochet stitch for each loop on the inner edge (i.e. 1 dc (sc) into a group of 2 loops, 1 ch) and 2 crochet stitches for each loop on the outer edge (i.e. 1 dc (sc) into a group of 2 loops, 3 ch).

Fig 21 Working a curve

SUGGESTED USES FOR DECORATIVE BRAIDS

The use of crochet headings not only produces a wider braid, but gives strength to the loops so that it is possible and often necessary to use a wider foundation braid than is advisable for the simpler braids. The addition of an extra yarn invites bold and colourful handling to make a braid that can be used as a special feature.

MAKING A SAMPLE

It is worth while taking a little time and patience to make a sample. This will almost certainly prove to be time-saving, produce a better design and give a crisp, neat end product rather than a braid which has become limp from frequent adjustments. The following hints are given as guide lines.

1 Choose the yarn and hairpin width taking into consideration whether the loops are to be twisted or taken up into groups and therefore need longer foundation loops.

2 Work a small sample length of 12 loops.

3 Choose a possible heading yarn and work the heading, adjusting until the braid lies flat.

4 Use a critical eye to decide whether the width, yarns and colours are effective.

5 When a satisfactory result is obtained measure the number of loops within 2.5 cm (1 in) in order to calculate the number of loops required for the finished length (diagram 28).

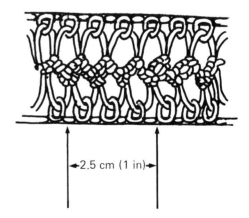

◄—2.5 cm (1 in)—►

Diag 28 Making a hairpin braid sample

Diagrams 29a, 29b
Edgings on bed linens and towels in pastel colours for feminine prettiness.

Diagrams 30a, 30b
Broad colourful braids in thicker yarns for bands on cushions, curtains and blinds.

Diagrams 31a, 31b, 31c
Bold braids on belts, braces and bags (guitar and camera straps). Choose firm yarns for good surface texture. For fastenings use clasps rather than buckles.

Diagram 32
Use on a sundress or camisole. Work firm headings as the edges will take a lot of strain during wear.

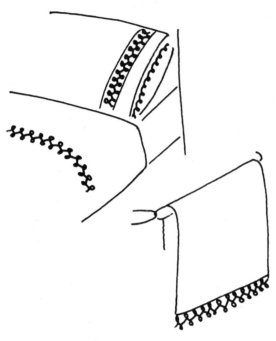

Diag 29a, 29b Edgings for bed linen and towels

Diag 30a, 30b Decorative braids for cushions and curtains

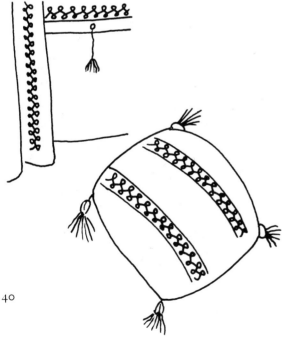

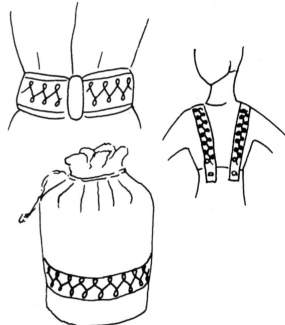

Diag 31a, 31b, 31c Decorative braids for belts, braces and bags

Diag 32 A camisole edging

Diagram 33

A sleeve insertion on a special blouse. The high collar uses the same braid with the addition of a treble heading on both edges threaded with a very narrow ribbon. Working instructions can be found with figure 22.

Diagrams 34a, 34b

Curved braids showing two ways to highlight a yoke. The sweater yoke trimming is stitched down. This can also be echoed with a straight band around the lower edge. The edging on the low-cut yoke must have a firm heading as explained for the sundress.

Figure 22

Shows in close up detail the sleeve insertion described in diagram 33. The working details are as follows:

Yarn: a fine 3-ply courtelle crepe to match the polyester jersey fabric.

Hook: 3.00 mm (D3)

Hairpin: 2.5 cm (1 in)

Braid: variation No. 5 (figure 7)

Heading: 1 dc (sc) 4 ch into each loop

WORKING A FRILL

If the inner edge of the curved braid is pulled straight the fullness of the outer edge is increased, resulting in a plain frill. The following instructions use several techniques already mastered to make very pretty frilled and flounced edgings.

PREPARING THE BRAID

Work the foundation braid first. This must be about double the length required to allow for fullness. The tension is given with each pattern so that the number of loops needed can be calculated.

COTTON FRILL (FIGURE 23)

This dainty frill is worked in a fine crochet cotton and is ideal for a pram pillowslip or a special handkerchief.

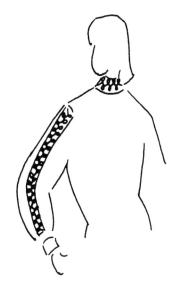

Diag 33 A sleeve insertion

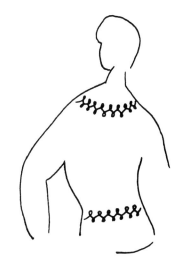

Diag 34a, 34b Curved braids for yokes

41

Fig 22 (top) A sleeve insertion   **Fig 23 (middle)** A cotton frill

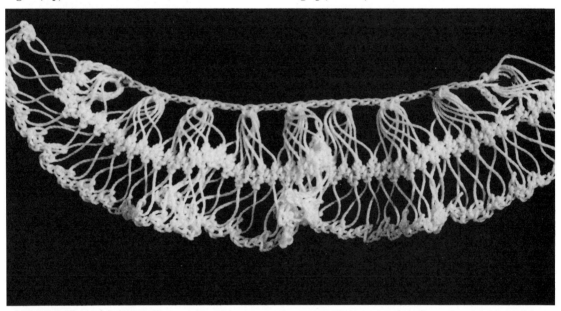

Fig 24 (bottom) A silky flounce

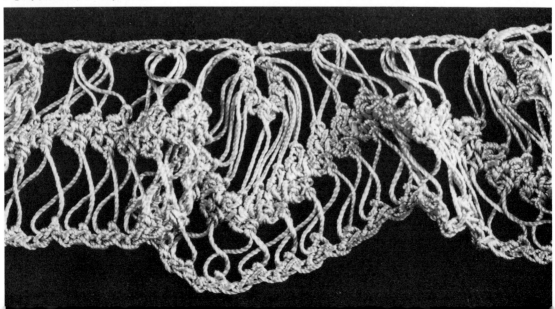

Details

No. 40 crochet cotton. 1.00 mm (Steel 9) crochet hook, 20 mm (¾ in) hairpin. Using the basic braid 20 lps = 2.5 cm (1 in) after gathering. For a 22 cm (9 in) square handkerchief work 720 lps.

Method

Work into twisted loops throughout.

The gathered edge: into a grp of 5 lps work 1 dc (sc), 3 ch. Repeat to the end.

The heading: into each lp work 1 dc (sc), 3 ch. Repeat to the end.

FLOUNCE (FIGURE 24)

When worked in a silky or Lurex yarn this deeper frill makes an attractive accessory for an evening dress or sweater. This example has an interesting method of making the flounce whereby 9 loops are formed into a ring to make the fullness. This treatment also causes the dip on the outer edge.

Details

Rayon or fine Lurex yarn. 1.50 mm (Steel 7) crochet hook, 40 mm (1½ in) hairpin. Using No. 1 braid, i.e. 2 dc (sc) into the left loop, 15 lps = 2.5 cm (1 in).

Method

Make a foundation braid having multiples of 3 lps.

The gathered edge: into a twisted grp of 3 lps (1 dc (sc), 4 ch) twice. 1 dc (sc) into each of the next 9 lps, sl st into the 1st dc (sc) (of these 9) to form a ring, 4 ch. Repeat from the beginning.

Heading: into each twisted lp, 1 dc (sc), 2 ch. Repeat to the end.

WORKING A FRINGE

Decorative fringes add a distinctive touch to many personal and home accessories. Hairpin crochet provides the needle worker with the means to make a fringe that will be exactly right in width, colour, texture and decorative qualities. They are very easy to make.

PREPARING THE FRINGE FOUNDATION BRAID

To produce a well balanced fringe choose a wide hairpin, at least 2.5 cm (1 in). Work close to one prong, instead of down the middle, so that the loops on one side will be twice as long as the other (diagram 35). If there is difficulty in keeping the work even, a hairpin loom can be adapted by inserting a knitting needle inside the 2 prongs. The braid will then be worked against the needle (diagram 36). To work the foundation braid cast on and work the short loop first.

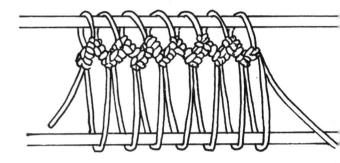

Diag 35 Working a hairpin fringe

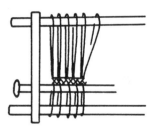

Diag 36 An improvised fringe hairpin

BEDSPREAD FRINGE (FIGURE 25)

Details

Finished depth 50 mm (2 in). Use a wider hairpin for a deeper fringe. Aran type yarn or thick knitting cotton according to the bedspread fabric. 4.50 mm (H8) crochet hook, 50 mm (2 in) hairpin. Basic braid was used for the sample.

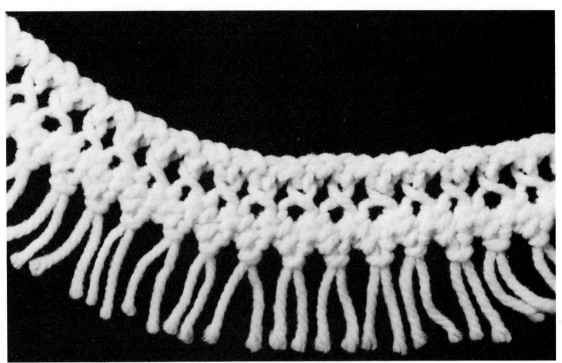

Fig 25 (top) A bedspread fringe   **Fig 26 (bottom)** A lampshade fringe

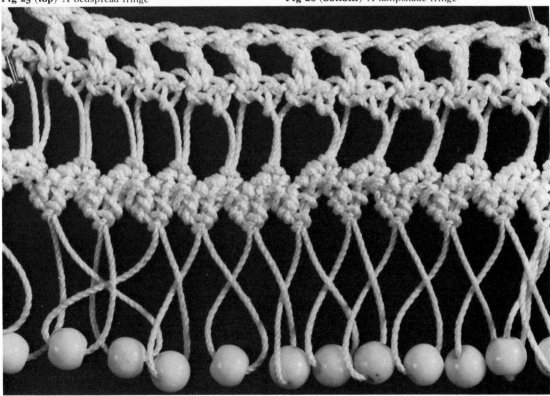

Method
Heading: working into the short lps, 1 dc (sc) into each twisted lp. Work the dc (sc) very loosely, or if preferred make a ch between each dc (sc). Cut the loops to finish.

LAMPSHADE FRINGE (FIGURE 26)

The use of beads for this fringe is optional. Apart from the decorative appeal their weight does help the loops to hang well especially when a finer yarn is used.

Details
Finished depth 4 cm (1½ in). No. 10 crochet cotton or rayon. 1.50 mm (Steel 7) crochet hook, 25 mm (1 in) hairpin. 5 beads per 2.5 cm (1 in). Braid No. 1 (2 dc (sc) into the left lp) was used for the sample.

Method
If beads are used these are threaded on to the yarn before starting the foundation braid, otherwise make a fringe foundation braid ready for the heading.

Making the braid: cast on and work 1 short lp. Turn. Bring 1 bead up to lie at the front of the pin between the prongs. Work 1 ch so that the bead is held in the long lp just made. Continue, bringing the beads up for the long lps only.

Heading 1st row: 1 dc (sc), 1 ch, into each short lp. Repeat to end.

2nd row: 1 tr (dc), 1 ch, into each dc (sc). Repeat to the end.

A narrow ribbon can be threaded through the heading.

ADDING FURTHER ROWS OF HEADING

If a deeper heading is planned, consideration must be given to the final balance so that the crochet does not overwhelm the fringe. A simple guide line is ⅓ depth of heading to ⅔ depth of loop. Therefore, if extra rows of heading are anticipated, use a much wider fringe braid. If planned carefully the result will be well worth the effort.

IDEAS FOR FRINGES

Diagram 37a
Use tubular rayon cord (rat-tail) often sold for macramé, for waste-bin and large lampshade fringes or on ethnic jerkins.

Diagram 37b
A deep decorative heading and fringe around a plain fabric shawl.

Diag 37a, 37b Using fringes on jerkins and shawls

FOUR SIMPLE BELTS SHOWN ON THE BACK JACKET

From the top.
(1) *Narrow belt in bronze lurex yarn 20 mm (¾ in) wide.* Work a basic braid to the exact waist measurement with a plain heading 1 dc (sc), 1 ch. Thread 1 m (1 yd) of russian braid through the loops down each side leaving the long ends to tie.

(2) *Broad belt in wools 50 mm (2 in) wide.* A variation of the first belt. Work a basic braid in a chunky yarn to the waist measurement with a twisted loop heading 1 dc (sc), 1 ch using double knitting wool. Thread long lengths of rug yarn through the loops leaving the ends to tie.

(3) *Raffia type belt using two lengths of basic braid, finished width 4 cm (1½ in).* Work 2 lengths 20 mm (¾ in) wide to the correct length. Join together by placing one braid on top of the other, sl st loosely through both loops. Fasten with a clasp.

(4) *Appliqué belt in silver lurex yarn, finished width 50 mm (2 in).* Work a basic foundation braid 40 mm (1½ in) with a heading of rayon yarn and twisted loops: 1 dc (sc) into a grp of 4 lps, 3 ch, (1 dc (sc) into 1 lp, 3 ch) three times. Repeat. Stitch to the belt.

II

HAIRPIN CROCHET FABRICS

6

JOINING THE BRAIDS TOGETHER

All the braids previously described, with or without headings, can be joined together to produce a variety of lacy fabrics ranging from delicate table mats to scarves, shawls and blankets. There are two ways to join the braid, firstly by using extra yarn and secondly by using cable joins which interlace the loops together.

JOINS USING EXTRA YARN

The familiar basic braid is used to show several methods of making the joins involving the use of extra yarn. This again is shown in a contrasting colour for easier identification. Whether to use one, two or even three colours is entirely a personal choice.

PREPARATION FOR JOINING

Making the foundation braids

As the work will now need several lengths of braid it is useful to mark the beginning of each braid so that it is easily recognised. Before starting the foundation braids tie an overhand knot at the end of the yarn as used in sewing. This is a quick easy way to avoid wasting time scrutinising or guessing which end is which. Allow long enough loops on these braids so that the open quality of the fabric will not be spoilt. Make 2 short lengths of foundation braid for practice; for the following samples use a 20 mm ($\frac{3}{4}$ in) hairpin with No. 10 crochet cotton except

where stated. Remember to start the joins at the casting-on end to allow for adjustements.

Handling the braids to be joined

Place one braid on top of the other with the loops of the back braid a little higher than the front braid and hold in the normal crochet position. Take care that the braids do not become twisted whilst working the join.

WORKING THE JOINS

Join 1 (figure 27)

Double crochet (sc) gives a very close, ridged join. Hold the braids as described.

    1 dc (sc) into the 1st back lp. 1 dc (sc) into the 1st front lp. Continue working into the alternate braids.

Join 2 (figure 28) Chevron style (a)

Both foundation braids have headings on each side. These are worked first.

    Heading (shown in grey): 1 dc (sc) into a group of 2 lps, 4 ch. Repeat.

    Joining (shown in white): 1 dc (sc) into the 1st 4 ch space of the 1st braid, 2 ch. 1 dc (sc) into the 1st 4 ch space of the 2nd braid, 2 ch. Continue working alternately.

Join 3 (figure 29) Chevron style (b)

The foundation braids do not have a heading, the twisting and joining being made in one operation. Work into groups of 2 twisted loops throughout.

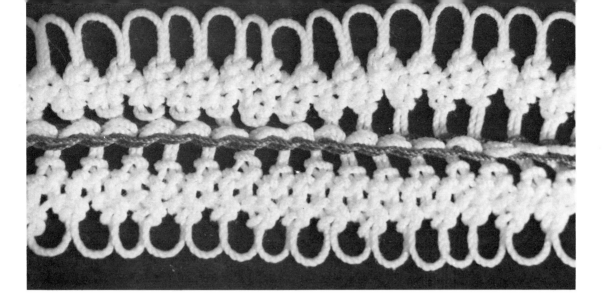

Fig 27 Join 1. Double crochet join (sc)
Fig 28 Join 2. Chevron style (a)

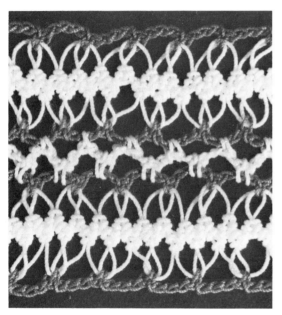

1 dc (sc) into the 1st group of the 1st braid, 2 ch. 1 dc (sc) into the 1st group of the 2nd braid, 2 ch. Continue working alternately.

Join 4 (figure 30)
This join is made in two stages. The heading is worked on the 1st braid, then the heading of the 2nd braid and the joining are worked in one operation. Work into groups of 2 twisted loops throughout.

1st braid heading: 1 dc (sc), 5 ch into each grp.

2nd braid: *1 dc (sc) into the 1st group, 2 ch, sl st into the 3rd stitch of the 1st 5 ch on the 1st braid, 2 ch. Repeat from *.

Fig 29 Join 3. Chevron style (b)

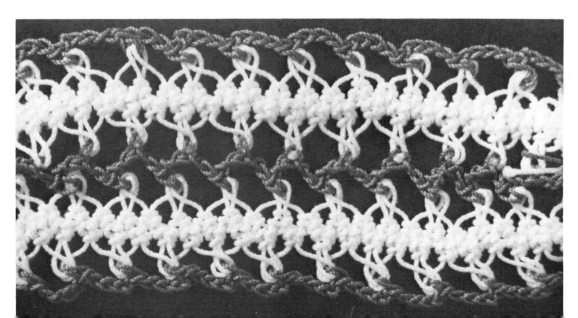

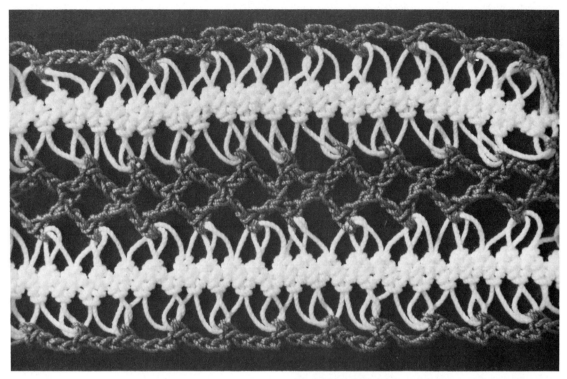

Fig 30 (top) Join 4. Chain lace style   **Fig 31 (bottom)** Join 5. Variation of join 4

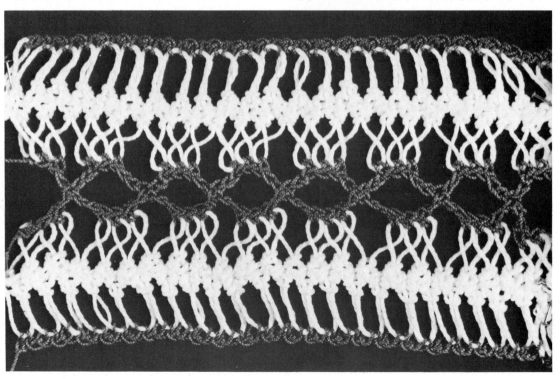

To add the 3rd and successive braids work the heading on the bottom side of the 2nd braid, then work the heading and joining on the 3rd braid.

Join 5 (figure 31)
This is a variation of join 4; the join is worked in the same manner, but the loops are taken up singly in blocks of 3. The foundation braids need multiples of 3 loops using a 50 mm (2 in) hairpin. The loops are twisted throughout.

1st braid: 1 dc (sc) into each of 3 lps, 5 ch. Repeat.

2nd braid: 1 dc (sc) into each of 3 lps, 2 ch, sl st into the 3rd of the 1st 5 ch on the 1st braid, 2 ch. Repeat.

Join 6 (figure 32)
This picot join is worked in a similar manner to join 5. Work into groups of 2 twisted loops throughout.

1st braid heading: 1 dc (sc), 3 ch into each group.

2nd braid: *1 dc (sc) into the 1st group, 3 ch, 1 sl st into the 1st dc (sc) on the 1st braid, 3 ch, sl st into the 1st dc (sc) on the 2nd braid (long picot now made) 3 ch. Repeat from *.

Join 7 (figure 33)
This shell join follows the same principle as join 5 in that the joins are made at the dc (sc). A wider braid is essential as the loops are taken up in groups of 4. The foundation braids should have multiples of 4 loops using a 50 mm (2 in) hairpin.

1st braid heading: 1 dc (sc) into the 1st group, 6 ch, 1 sl st into the spine, 6 ch. Repeat.

2nd braid: *1 dc (sc) into the 1st group, 1 sl st into the 1st dc (sc) of the 1st braid, 6 ch, 1 sl st into the spine of the 2nd braid, 6 ch. Repeat from *.

The 6 ch may need adjusting depending upon the yarn used.

Fig 32 Join 6. A picot join

Fig 33 Join 7. A shell join

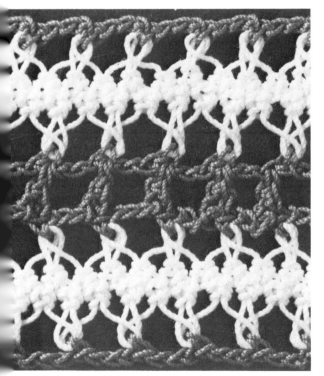

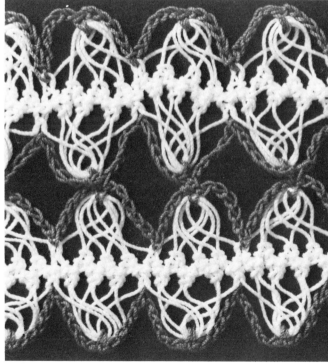

CABLE JOINS

This method differs in that the loops of adjoining braids are slip stitched together without using extra yarns, resulting in a plaited effect. When trying this method for the first time it is helpful to use two braids of contrasting colours, in fact the intertwining colours or shades can be very attractive. Note that rayon or any other type of slippery yarn is not suitable for cable joins. The braids are 20 mm ($\frac{3}{4}$ in) wide.

ONE-TO-ONE CABLING (FIGURE 34)

Holding the two braids side by side the loops are taken up alternately from each braid and drawn through each other as follows.

1 Insert the hook into the 1st lp of the 1st braid and then into the 1st lp of the 2nd braid. Draw the 1st lp through the 2nd lp.

2 Take up the next lp on the 1st braid and draw through the lp on the hook.
  Continue taking alternate lps in this manner to the end. Fasten off the last lp with a short length of yarn.

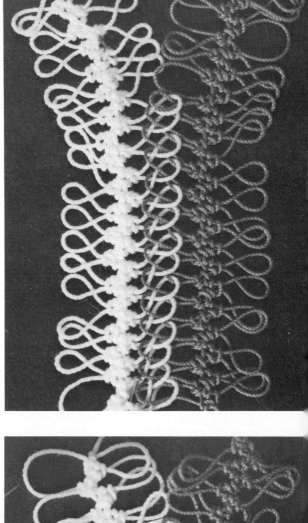

TWO-TO-TWO CABLING (FIGURE 35)

This example shows the loops taken up in groups of 2 and is worked in exactly the same way. When taking up groups of loops the use of a larger hook will be more efficient.

Figure 36
Shows a portion of fabric using the 2–2 cable method. It is worked in fine knitting cotton with 40 mm ($1\frac{1}{2}$ in) braids.

To take up groups of 3 loops or more will only be possible with wider braids. This method obviously takes up the width of the loops and therefore the finished width of a braid will be much narrower, a fact that must be taken into consideration when planning a piece of work. If a thicker yarn is used the foundation braid must be worked on a wider pin.

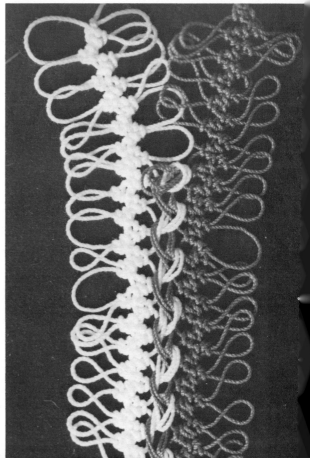

Fig 34 One-to-one cable join
Fig 35 Two-to-two cable join

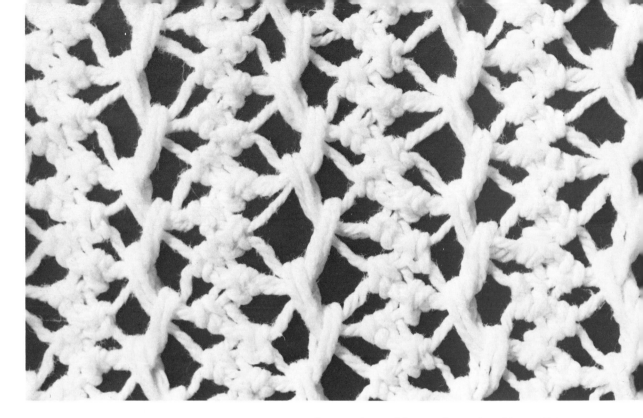

Fig 36 A hairpin fabric using the cable join

DECORATIVE BRAIDS USING JOINS

Although joins are used mainly for the making of fabrics they can also be used to good effect on a very special border.

EXAMPLE

Join 5 (figure 31) shows 2 braids with a central join. The outer loops have a simple heading of 1 dc (sc), 1 ch into each untwisted loop, making an interesting braid. This could be taken a step further with another row of crochet.

JOINING CORNERS

When joining together braids which include corners the 2nd braid will need to be longer than the 1st braid and must be calculated accordingly. The centre loop of the corner group on the 1st braid will be joined to the corner group of the 2nd braid (figure 37). The number of loops taken up in the corner groups remains the same for the first and all subsequent rounds, but the number of loops along the sides will increase. This is calculated quite easily by adding on extra number of corner loops to each side.

HOW TO CALCULATE THE LOOPS

1 Work the 1st braid as shown in chapter 5.

2 Note the number of corner lps; e.g. 5.

3 Note the number of lps worked for 1 side, e.g. 25. Add the number of corner lps, 5, total 30 lps.

4 For the 2nd braid add an extra number of corner lps (5) to the previous total (30) giving a sum of 35 lps of 1 side and 1 corner for the 2nd braid.

5 To complete the square multiply by 4 (140 lps).

6 If further rounds are needed simply add 5 lps (or the corner lp number) to each side.

Remember, wider braids will require more corner lps.

WORK A SAMPLE CORNER (FIGURE 37)

This narrow chevron join is the simplest way of

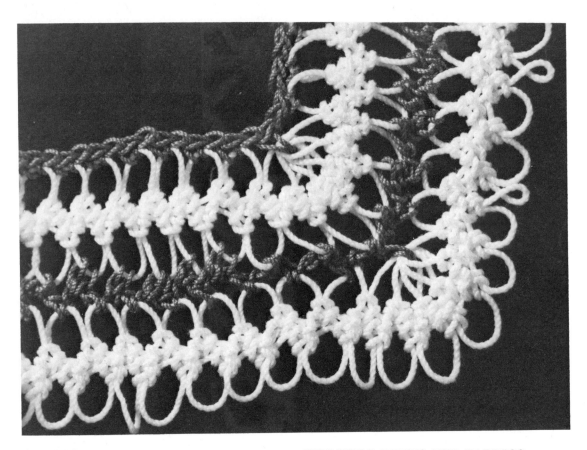

Fig 37 Joining corners

joining corners and will give confidence to the worker prior to using any other join.

　　1st braid: Make a braid of 25 lps. Work down one side (1 dc (sc) into 1 lp, 1 ch) 10 times, 1 dc (sc) into a group of 5 lps, (1 ch, 1 dc (sc) into 1 lp) 10 times.

　　It is useful to tie a marker thread on to the middle loop of the 5 corner group so that it is easily identified when joining on the second braid.

　　2nd braid: Make a braid of 30 lps (note this is 5 more than the 1st braid). Using extra yarn work 1 dc (sc), 1 ch into the 1st lp of the 1st braid, 1 dc (sc) into the 1st lp of the 2nd braid, continue working alternately into each band until the marker thread is reached. Take up 5 lps from the 2nd braid with 1 dc (sc). Continue along the 2nd side with 1 ch, 1 dc (sc) into alternate braids.

WORKING HINTS FOR FABRICS

BRAID WIDTHS

Hairpin fabrics owe their main attraction to the open, lacy quality of the loops. It is possible to join narrow braids together to produce a close fabric, but as this type of result can be achieved from ordinary crochet it is not really worth doing something that is not easily recognised as hairpin crochet. Nor should the loops be made too long, giving a weak, floppy join. If the loops are to be twisted, taken up into groups or joined by the cable method a fairly long loop will be necessary.

MAKING A WELL-SHAPED FABRIC

Hairpin braids have a diagonal structure which may become exaggerated when they are joined. A fabric using several braid lengths may become distorted, so it is advisable, when joining, to alternate the taking up of the first loop or group in order to keep the fabric square. This is done as follows (diagram 38):

1 Join lengths 1 and 2 by picking up the 1st lp on No. 1 length first.

2 Join lengths 2 and 3 by picking up the 1st lp on No. 3 length first.

3 Join lengths 3 and 4 by picking up the 1st lp on No. 3 length first.

4 Join lengths 4 and 5 by picking up the 1st lp on No. 5 length first.

5 Continue in this manner, alternating the picking up of the 1st lp of the attached length and then the unattached length.

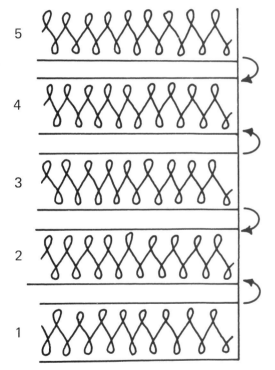

Diag 38 Joining several braids to form a fabric

FINISHING THE EDGES

The looped edges can be left to give a fringed effect or can be finished with any of the headings shown in chapter 5. The joined edges may be finished in any of the following ways.

Diagram 39
The crochet heading chosen for the looped edges can be used on all sides using judgement to space the stitches across the joined edges and also at the corners. The loose ends must then be run in.

Diagram 40
Binding with a suitable ribbon, tape or fabric will neaten the ends and hide the loose ends. This method is especially suitable for baby blankets.

Diagram 41
The loose ends can be left and further lengths of yarn knotted into the loops and spines to form a fringe.

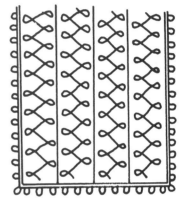

Diag 39 A crochet edging around a hairpin fabric

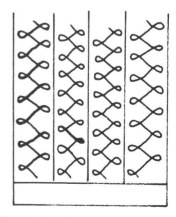

Diag 40 Binding the edges of a hairpin fabric

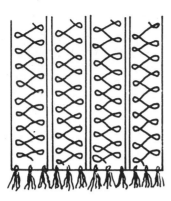

Diag 41 Fringing the ends of a hairpin fabric

To make a knotted fringe (diagrams 42a, 42b, 42c)

1 Cut lengths of yarn more than double the desired finished length.

2 Take approximately 3 lengths together, depending on the thickness of the fringe, and double them in half (diagram 42a).

3 Insert a larger hook into the hairpin fabric and draw the folded length halfway through (diagram 42b).

4 Draw the cut ends through this loop just formed and tighten (diagram 42c).

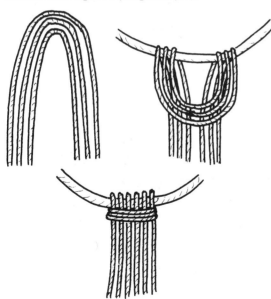

Diag 42a, 42b, 42c Making a knotted fringe

This must be done with care, never heavily to distort the loops. Pin out the piece first. Use a damp press for cotton and pure wool. Synthetic yarns should only be pressed lightly with a dry iron if at all.

In order to retain the full textural effect, especially with heavier yarns, the fabric can be dampened, pinned to shape on a board and left to dry.

SUGGESTED USES FOR HAIRPIN FABRICS

The following notes give advice on the yarns and techniques most suitable for a representative range of articles made with hairpin fabrics. Some of the suggestions also include full details for making the required fabrics. These can be adjusted or developed at the worker's discretion, e.g. the details for a place mat can be doubled for a table runner, or details for a stole reduced for a scarf.

FINE HAIRPIN FABRICS

These are particularly attractive when used for home accessories such as table settings. For a special baby's or child's dress the home dress-maker could use a fine hairpin fabric for a yoke or pockets lined with the dress fabric.

Suitable yarns
Crochet cottons Nos 10 and 20, Perle cotton No. 5 and fine knitting cotton. All these will produce a fairly substantial fabric which will stay put when in use providing the loops are not too long. It is difficult to assess how much yarn will be required as this depends on the yarn and the density of the fabric. As a rough guide, calculate on the basis that 2 balls of crochet cotton will be required for one place mat measuring approximately 30×38 cm (12×15 in).

Suggested uses
The following suggestions for household accessories can all be made up exactly as shown in

the sample joins 1 to 7 using No. 10 crochet cotton, a 1.50 mm (Steel 7) crochet hook and the hairpin width given with the sample. Simply work the foundation braids to the required length, join and finish the edges with a suitable heading.

The notes with the sketches offer suggestions for alternative yarns.

Diagram 43
Fine knitting cotton makes a very practical fabric for place mats, trolley- or traycloths; shown with the braids placed horizontally.

Details for a cabled braid mat measuring
38 × 24 cm (15 × 9 in)
25 g (1 oz) fine knitting cotton. 2.00 mm (B1) crochet hook, 40 mm (1½ in) hairpin. Work 10 lengths of basic braid with approximately 65 loops. Join with 2 to 2 cabling. Edge with a plain substantial border of 3 rows of double crochet (sc). See figure 36 for a close-up view of the fabric.

Diagram 44
Table runners and cheval sets look decorative in perle cotton, or a glossy rayon shown here with the braids running across the width. Remember that a slippy yarn is not successful with cable joins.

Diagram 45
A hairpin fabric placed over a plain rigid lampshade will show a well-designed pattern to perfection. This can be worked in either perle cotton, craft cotton or even thin string for a bold textural quality. Note that a drum lampshade is recommended; a conical shape would present shaping problems. The fabric should fit tightly and be secured at the top and bottom of the shade with either stitches or adhesive.

WOLLEN-TYPE FABRICS

These larger scale fabrics open up all kinds of possibilities from simple quickly made scarves and stoles to eye-catching afghans. Very wide hairpins up to 100 mm (4 in) can be used, but take care that the finer yarns do not look too

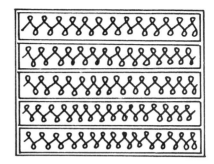

Diag 43 Hairpin fabric table mats

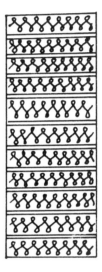

Diag 44 Hairpin fabric table runners

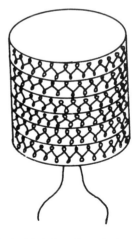

Diag 45 Hairpin fabric for a lampshade

spindly. Take the opportunity to use vibrant colours, or gently shade the colour through the braids.

The yarns

As the range, density and weight of yarns varies so widely with each manufacturer the following hints must only be used as a guide as to the type and amount suitable for various projects.

Mohair and brushed synthetic yarns

These are very easy to work and require surprisingly little yarn. They are at their best made on wide hairpins using the basic braid and only a simple join. Even though this results in a very open fabric they do not loose shape and are very warm to wear.

Details for a scarf measuring 150 × 30 cm (60 × 12 in)

75 g (3 oz) Mohair yarn. 6.00 mm (I9) crochet hook. 80 mm (3 in) hairpin. Work 3 lengths of the basic braid. Use join No. 1 working chains between the double crochets if required. A stole can be worked in the same way.

Double knitting, Aran and chunky yarns

These can also be worked on wide hairpins and will show off a bold decorative fabric using twisted groups and cable joins. As these types of yarn differ widely it is difficult to assess a certain quantity. In such cases make up a sample then use up one ball of wool and make a judgement based on the result.

Details for an afghan measuring 150 × 100 cm (60 × 40 in)

900 g (36 oz) Aran type yarn. 5.00 mm (H8) crochet hook, 100 mm (4 in) hairpin. Work 20 lengths of the basic braid. Use a two-to-two cable join.

A cushion cover 35 cm (14 in) square can be made in the same way using 4 lengths of braid. Allow 300 g (12 oz). Work both sides, finishing the edges with a narrow braid of the same yarn.

Four ply and baby yarn

Fine wools make up into soft lacy fabrics and are most suited to twists and finely worked joins. Beware of over-long loops (no more than 50 mm (2 in) wide) as they will crumple when in use, destroying the delicacy of the design. They are ideal for stoles, baby shawls or pram covers.

Details for a stole measuring 180 × 64 cm (72 × 25 in)

250 g (10 oz) baby wool. 3.00 mm (C2) crochet hook, 50 mm (2 in) hairpin. Work 10 lengths of braid and join with No. 5 picot join. Work a heading all the way round.

For a baby blanket work half a stole and edge with a narrow braid.

7
HAIRPIN FAN BRAIDS AND FABRICS

This form of hairpin crochet is perhaps one of the most popular and prettiest methods of using a basic braid. As for other braids with headings, a foundation braid is worked and finished off first. The fans are made in the working of the heading which takes up a large group of loops to form a fan.

WORKING FAN BRAIDS AND JOINS

PREPARING THE BRAID

A wide braid gives a better result and it will be necessary to work a basic length of between a third to a half more than the required length. The samples have fans of 12 loops, but larger or smaller groups can be used. The braid is 2.5 cm (1 in) wide with 48 loops on each side. Longer lengths will need multiples of 12 loops. It is advisable to study the relevant photograph before and during working.

FAN BRAID 1 (FIGURE 38)

When working the heading the loops are taken up in groups of 12.

1st side: 1 dc (sc) into the base of the 1st lp (i.e. into the spine), 6 ch. *1 dc (sc) into a grp of 12 lps, 6 ch. 1 tr (dc) into the spine immediately after the last lp, 6 ch. Repeat from * ending with 1 dc (sc) into a grp of 12 lps, 6 ch, 1 tr (dc) into the end of the spine.

Fig 38 Fan braid 1

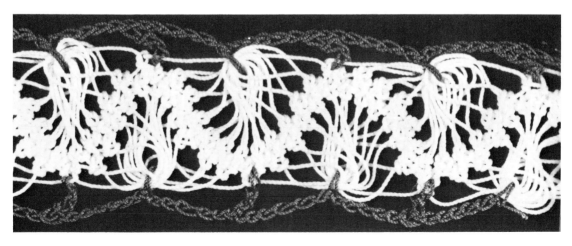

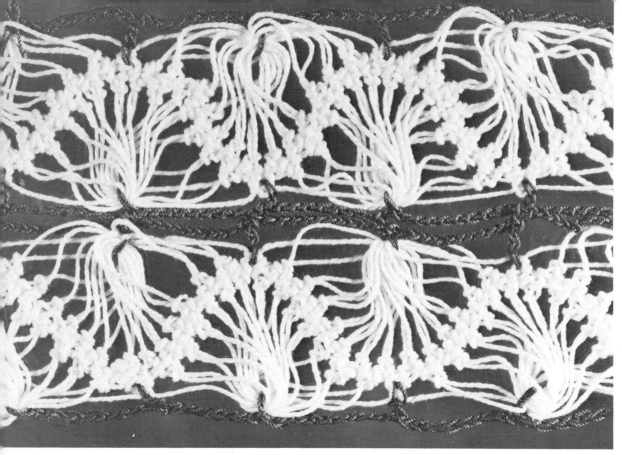

Fig 39 (top) Joining fan braid 1   **Fig 40 (bottom)** Fan braid 2

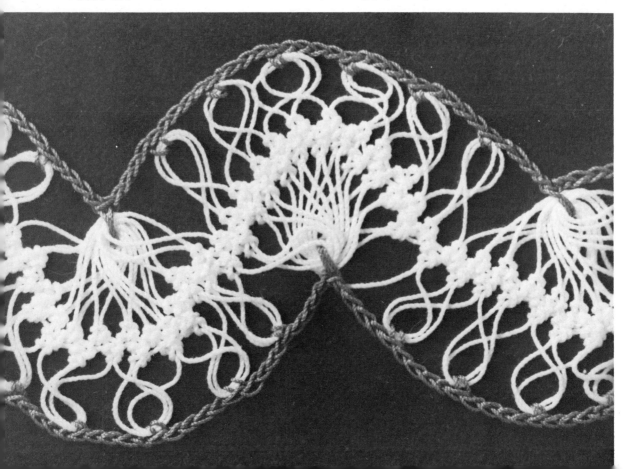

2nd side: 1 dc (sc) into a grp of 6 lps, 6 ch. *1 tr (dc) into the spine, 6 ch. 1 dc (sc) into a grp of 12 lps, 6 ch. Repeat from * but ending with 1 dc (sc) into a grp of 6 lps.

TO JOIN (FIGURE 39)

When the braids are joined the fans and the tips of the spine meet. This follows the same method as join 4 in chapter 6 where the heading and joining of the 2nd braid is worked in one operation.

1st braid: work as explained above.

2nd braid: 1 dc (sc) into the 1st grp of 6 lps, sl st into the corresponding 1st $\frac{1}{2}$ fan on the 1st braid, 6 ch. 1 tr (dc) into the spine of the 2nd braid, 1 sl st into the 1st tr (dc) on the 1st braid, 6 ch. 1 dc (sc) into a grp of 12 lps, sl st into same place on the 1st braid. Continue in this manner to the end.

Work the 2nd side of the 2nd braid as given for the 1st side of the 1st braid.

To make a 50 mm (2 in) wide braid take up 14 lps for the fans. The foundation braid will then require multiples of 14 lps. Adjust the chains where necessary.

FAN BRAID 2 (FIGURE 40)

To form the fans the loops are again taken up in groups of 12 but the loops on the opposite side are taken up in groups of 2 to form a gentle curve. Work into the twisted loops throughout.

1st side: *1 dc (sc) into a grp of 12 lps (4 ch, 1 dc (sc) into a grp of 2 lps) 6 times, 4 ch. Repeat from *.

2nd side: Work as the 1st side, but starting with (1 dc (sc) into a grp of 2, 4 ch) 6 times. 1 dc (sc) into a grp of 12 lps, 4 ch.

TO JOIN (FIGURE 41)

This uses the picot join No. 5 in chapter 6. The braids interlock and the joins follow the curves. Crochet down both sides of the 1st braid. The heading and joining on the 2nd braid is worked together.

1 dc (sc) into a grp of 12 lps on the 2nd braid, 3 ch, 1 dc (sc) between the 3rd and 4th 2-lp grps on the curve of the 1st braid, 3 ch, sl st into the dc (sc) on the 2nd braid (picot made), 4 ch.

*1 dc (sc) into a grp of 2 on the 2nd braid, 3 ch, 1 dc (sc) into the next ch space on the 1st braid, 3 ch, sl st into the dc (sc) just made on the 2nd braid, 4 ch.

Repeat from * 6 times altogether then take up another grp of 12 lps on the 2nd braid, 4 ch. Repeat from * to the end. Work the 2nd side of the 2nd braid as explained for the 1st braid. Figure 41 shows this stage in progress.

FAN BRAID 3 (FIGURE 42)

This variation again takes up groups of 12 loops, but the opposite loops are taken up singly. Work into untwisted loops throughout.

1st side: *1 dc (sc) into a grp of 12 lps, (2 ch, 1 dc (sc) into 1 lp) 12 times, 2 ch. Work from * to the end.

2nd side: Work as the 1st side, but start with *(1 dc (sc) into 1 lp, 2 ch) 12 times. 1 dc (sc) into a grp of 12, 2 ch. Repeat from * to the end.

If the curve does not lie flat adjust the number of chains.

TO JOIN

This follows the same method as join 2 (chevron) in Chapter 6. Crochet down both sides of the braids first, shown in grey. The join is shown in white.

1 dc (sc) into the 1st grp of 12 on the 2nd strip, 3 ch. 1 dc (sc) between the 6th and 7th lps on the curve of the 1st strip, 3 ch. 1 dc (sc) into the next alternate ch space on the 2nd strip, 3 ch. Continue working 1 dc (sc), 3 ch into each alternate space on alternate braids.

MAKING A STRAIGHT JOINED EDGE

It will be noticed that these fan braids have rounded ends (figure 42). When making a fabric these can be exploited to give a scalloped edge. If a straight side edge is needed this can be made by working only half a fan at the start and finish of each braid. When starting the heading work 1 dc (sc) into a grp of 6 lps, then continue with the pattern to the last 6 lps which will be half a fan.

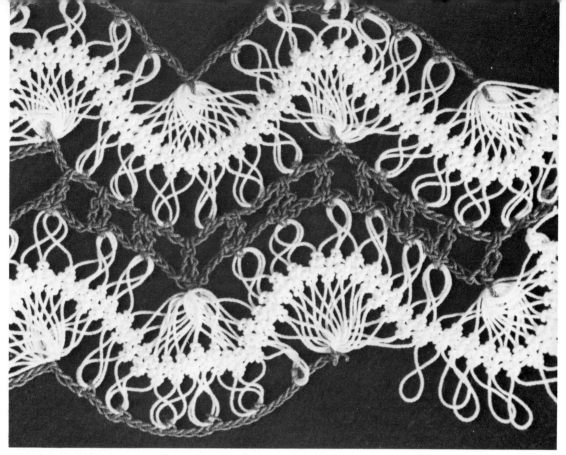

Fig 41 (top) Joining fan braid 2   **Fig 42 (bottom)** Fan braid 3

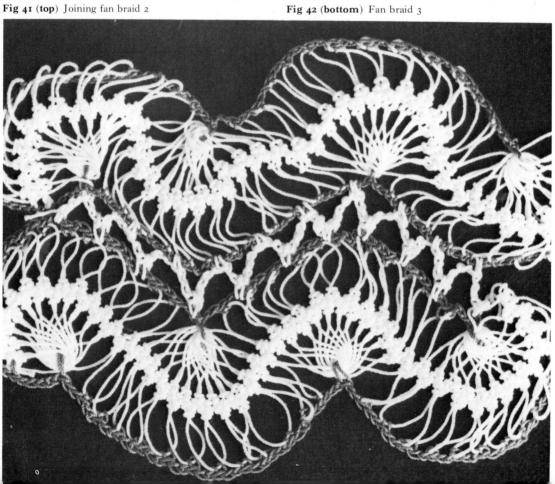

SUGGESTED USES FOR HAIRPIN FANS

Hairpin fan fabrics can be used for very special scarves, stoles, shawls or pram covers. Figure 43 shows a close-up view of a fan braid fabric made up into a scarf. This is a good example of the various effects possible when different yarns and colours are used.

A FAN BRAID SCARF (FIGURE 43) MEASURING
115 × 35 cm (44 × 15 in)

125 g (5 oz) double knitting yarn approximately. 4.00 (G6) crochet hook 80 mm (3 in) hairpin. The scarf has 4 lengths of fan braid 2. The fan braid produces a wavy edge along the length whilst the joined edges can be left as scallops with or without a fringe. To enlarge the scarf into a stole add 25 g (1 oz) of yarn for each additional braid.

FAN BRAIDS AS BORDERS

Although fan braids are mainly used for fabrics they can be used for borders.

Fig 43 A fan braid fabric

8

HAIRPIN CROCHET ROUNDS

The worker will now realise how versatile a length of hairpin braid can be and will appreciate why this form of crochet work was particularly popular for making doilies during the Victorian and Edwardian eras. A short length of foundation basic braid is all that is required for a simple round motif. It can then be developed in the same way as the braids with headings and joins.

A SIMPLE ROUND MOTIF (figure 44)

The samples throughout this chapter were worked with No. 10 crochet cotton and a 1.50 mm (Steel 7) crochet hook. A 20 mm ($\frac{3}{4}$ in) hairpin was used except where stated.

Fig 44 A round hairpin motif

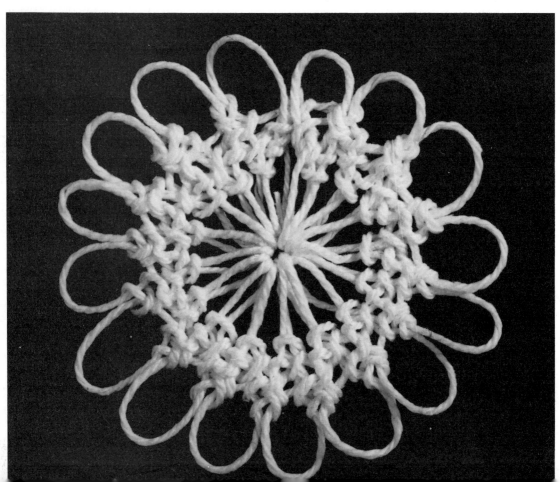

MAKING A BRAID RING

Using the basic braid work a length with 16 lps on each side. Do not fasten off. Remove the braid from the pin and form it into a ring, taking care not to twist it.

Join the ends by working a sl st well into the spine at the cast-on end.

Consider carefully the best place to work the sl st so that both ends of the spine meet evenly. Fasten off.

A round motif variation
Make a foundation fringe braid so that when the ring is joined a small compact centre will be ringed with longer loops.

JOINING THE INNER LOOPS

A gathered centre (figure 44)
Using a sewing needle and a strong matching thread run the needle through the inner lps making sure they all lie the same way. Draw up tightly, tie securely and cut the ends.

Fig 45 A hairpin wheel motif

A crochet centre (diagram 46)
Work 1 dc (sc) into each lp or grps of 2 lps, sl st into the 1st dc (sc). This forms a central hole and may require more braid lps.

An alternative crochet centre (diagram 47)
Take the lps up in 4 grps. For a motif with 16 lps work 1 dc (sc) into a grp of 4 lps, 4 times.

This small motif can now be used for appliqué in many attractive ways or developed further.

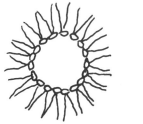

Diag 46 Hairpin round motif with a crochet centre
Diag 47 An alternate crochet centre

EDGING A ROUND MOTIF

This is worked as for braid headings, the only difference being that extra chains are needed between the loops to form a curve instead of a straight edge.

A WHEEL MOTIF USING A PLAIN CHAIN HEADING (FIGURE 45)

Using the basic motif with 16 lps work 1 dc (sc), 4 ch, into each lp, sl st into the 1st dc (sc) and fasten off. Adjust the number of chains if necessary.

DECORATIVE HEADINGS

Picot heading (diagram 48)
Worked as the picot heading shown in chapter 5 braid 10, but allowing extra chains. e.g. 1 dc (sc), 3 ch, sl st into the same dc (sc), 4 ch. Repeat all round joining with a sl st.

Shell edging (diagram 49)
A 2nd row of crochet shells is worked on to the wheel motif as follows: into each ch lp, 1 dc (sc), 1 htr (hdc), 1 tr (dc), 1 htr (hdc) 1 dc (sc). To finish make a sl st into the 1st dc (sc).

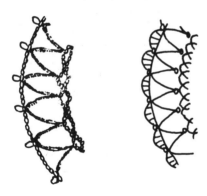

Diag 48 A picot edging for a round motif
Diag 49 A shell edging for a round motif

A cable heading (figure 46)
This type of heading is only successful with long loops, so the motif braid must be at least 50 mm (2 in) wide with a larger number of

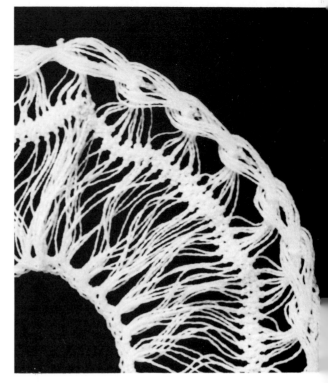

Fig 46 A cable heading for a round motif

loops. A softer yarn such as perle or fine knitting cotton is more suitable so that the loops can combine well when taken up in groups.

Figure 46 shows the loops of a 80 mm (3 in) wide braid taken up in grps of 5. A braid with multiples of 5 lps is therefore needed.

Method
Using a larger hook take up the lps in groups of 5, cable all round the outer edge. To complete the round tie the last grp over the 1st grp.

To hold the cabling firmly in place take extra yarn to work 1 dc (sc) round the stem of a 5 lp grp, 7 ch. Repeat all round, join to the 1st st dc (sc). The chains should lie hidden behind the cabling.

IDEAS FOR APPLIQUÉ MOTIFS

FOR GARMENTS

Here is a quick way to give clothes the individual touch.

Diag 50a, 50b, 50c Using hairpin motifs on clothes

Diagram 50a

Small daisies scattered on a child's dress. The motifs can be given yellow 'eyes' by using the crochet centre method shown in diagram 46.

Diagram 50b

A decorative spray with motifs of various sizes for use on an evening dress. The centres are gathered with a sequin stitched on top. Groups of single sequins complement the motifs. Couched stems are optional.

Diagram 50c

These large, bold motifs worked in wool look very pleasing if they are made with 2 or 3 strands of fine wool. Stitch to the shoulder of a sweater.

FOR ACCESSORIES

Diagram 51

An outsize motif on a bright workbasket lid using chunky wool. The inner loops are gathered and the outer loops stitched down. A larger wooden bead makes a knob.

Diagram 52

A double motif creates a sunflower. Make a large motif (30 mm ($1\frac{1}{4}$ in) hairpin) in thick crochet on knitting cotton and the small motif (10 mm ($\frac{1}{2}$ in) hairpin) in a finer, silky yarn to stitch in the centre. Appliqué on to bags, cushions or wall hangings.

Diagram 53

Wheel motifs for a broad belt. For casual wear use canvas webbing with colourful wheels and finished off with central beads or buttons.

Diag 51 An outsize motif for a basket lid

Diag 52 A large double sunflower motif

Diag 53 Hairpin motifs for a belt

67

9

FABRICS MADE FROM ROUNDS

JOINING WHEEL MOTIFS

The method used for this type of hairpin fabric
uses the same principle as that used for ordinary
crochet motifs. The first wheel motif is worked
complete with a plain chain heading. Thereafter
each motif is joined to its neighbour at 2 points
whilst working the heading.

HOW TO JOIN THE MOTIFS (DIAGRAM 54)

Work the 1st complete wheel motif. Refer to the
diagram throughout the joining process.

2nd motif: Work the heading as follows: (1 dc
(sc) 4 ch) into 13 lps. *1 dc (sc) into the next lp, 1
sl st into a dc (sc) of the 1st motif, 4 ch. Repeat
from * once more. The 2 motifs are now joined
together at 2 adjacent lps. Complete the heading
of the 2nd motif. Finish off.

3rd motif: Work the heading into 13 lps. On
the 1st motif miss 2 lps. Complete the 3rd motif
heading.

4th motif: This is joined in 2 places, firstly to
the 2nd motif and then to the 3rd motif. Work
the heading into 9 lps. On the 2nd motif miss 2
lps before the 1st join, then join on the 4th motif
at the next 2 lps. Work the heading into the next
2 lps then join to the 3rd motif missing 2 lps
after the previous join. Complete and finish off
(figure 47).

To add further motifs repeat the instructions
for motifs 3 and 4.

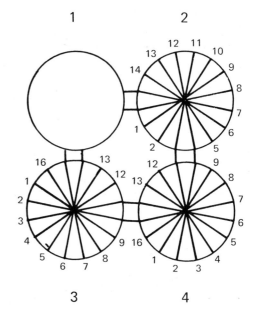

Diag 54 Joining 4 motifs together

FILLING THE CENTRAL SPACE (FIGURE 47)

With extra yarn work 1 dc (sc) into any dc (sc) in
the space, 5 ch. (1 tr (dc), 2 ch) into each of the 7
remaining dc (sc). Join with a sl st into the 3rd of
the 1st 5 ch. Finish off.

When the fabric is completed make a border
by working dc (sc) into the 2 outer lps with a ch
between. Note that all the motifs will now have

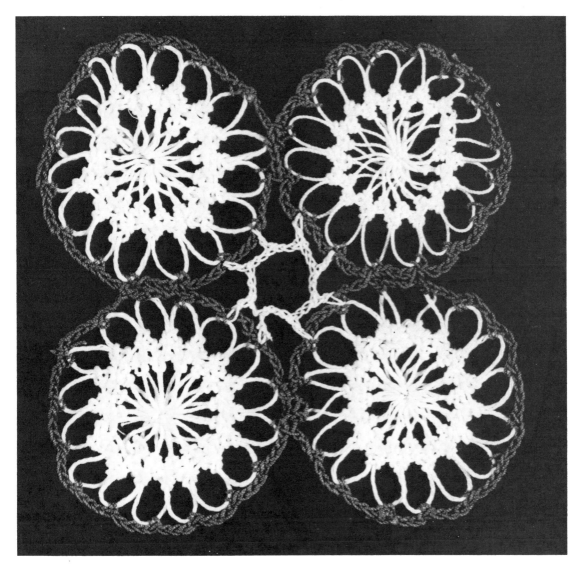

Fig 47 Four motifs joined together

2 lps free between each join. Add further rows of plain crochet trebles (dc) for strength and balance.

A MOHAIR ARMENIAN SHAWL (figures 48, 49)

This delightful antique shawl is an outstanding example of hairpin motif fabrics. On close inspection it is amazing to find that each 75 cm (3 in) diameter motif is made in a fine single strand of mohair with 60 loops. The centres are gathered whilst the outer loops are taken up in 3 loop groups with 1 dc (sc) and 3 ch. The joins connect at 3 adjacent loops, the spaces being filled with petal motifs which are made as large picots starting from the centre. The shawl is finished with a very narrow braid using 3 strands of mohair which is allowed to twist and is only connected to the main part at each join making a very interesting looped edge.

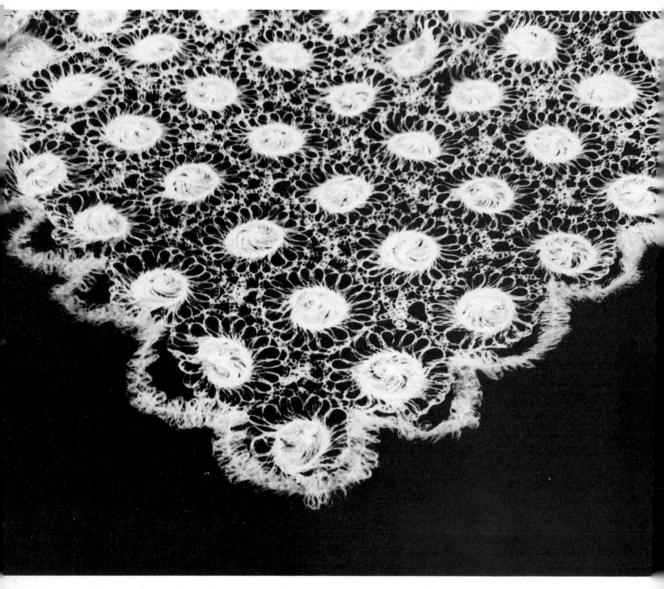

The shawl measures 120 cm (48 in) square with 13 × 13 motifs (169) and is as light as a cobweb. (By kind permission of the Rachel B. Kay Shuttleworth Collection.)

ENLARGING THE BASIC MOTIF

By using the round motif as a foundation it is possible to add further rounds by employing the joining methods shown in Chapter 6. It is obvious that each successive round must be

Fig 48 (**top**) A mohair Armenian shawl
Fig 49 (**right**) A close-up view of the Armenian shawl

larger; the simple principle being that each additional round requires double the number of loops of its predecessor, e.g. 1st round 20 lps, 2nd round 40 lps, 3rd round 80 lps.

When making the joins 1 loop of the 1st round is joined to 2 loops of the 2nd round. The chevron type join 3 shown in Chapter 6 is the most suitable.

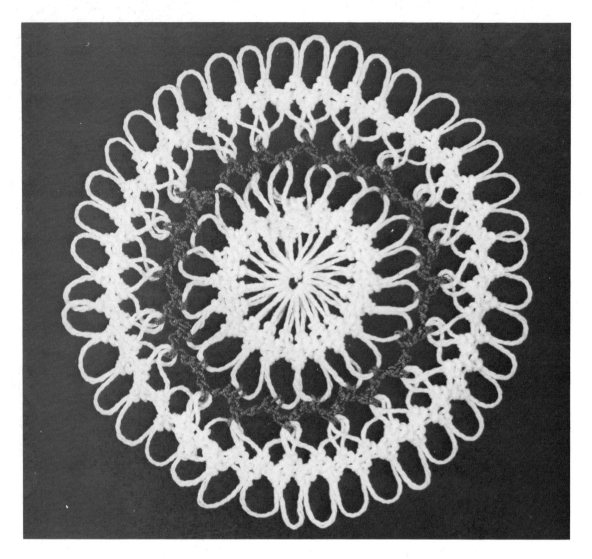

TO MAKE A DOILY 14 cm ($5\frac{1}{2}$ in) DIAMETER
(FIGURE 50)

The sample was worked with No. 10 crochet
cotton, 1.50 mm (Steel 7) crochet hook and
20 mm ($\frac{3}{4}$ in) hairpin.

Method
Make a central motif with 20 lps using the basic
braid.

1st round: Make a basic braid of 40 lps. Join
and finish off.

To join: Work into straight lps on the motif
and twisted lps on the 1st round. 1 dc (sc) into 1
lp on the motif, 2 ch. 1 dc (sc) into a 2-lp grp on

Fig 50 Working a doily

the 1st round. Repeat all round. Join with a sl st
into the 1st dc (sc).

For further rounds double the number of
loops and work in the same way.

USING THE ALTERNATIVE CHEVRON JOIN 2,
CHAPTER 6

Method
Make a central wheel motif with 20 lps and a
heading of 1 dc (sc), 4 ch.

1st round: Make a round of 40 lps with an

inner heading of 1 dc (sc), 6 ch. Check that the central motif will lie inside the 1st round with sufficient space for the joining chains.

To join: *1 dc (sc) into a ch space on the motif 2 ch, 1 dc (sc) into a ch space on the 1st round. Repeat.

USING WIDER BRAIDS FOR ROUNDS

If a wider braid is needed work more loops on the central motif. Use as many loops as possible so that the spine lies flat and the outer loops are not stretched when the ring is formed.

THE FINAL EDGING

Headings are worked as explained for the basic motif. If the cable edging is used, long floppy loops will be avoided by using a fringe foundation braid. Use a wider hairpin so that the small loops will be worked to match the loops of the previous round. The long outer loops will then be taken up by the cabling. To judge the width of the outer braid, the hairpin should be half as wide again as the previous round, e.g. from 25 mm (1 in) to 40 mm ($1\frac{1}{2}$ in).

IDEAS FOR DOILIES

DIAGRAM 55

Large doilies worked in thick yarns make very unusual round cushions. Use braids of at least 50 mm (2 in) wide. Line the cushion with a

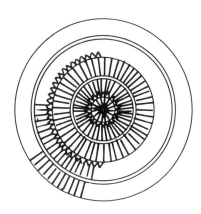

Diag 55 Round hairpin cushions

contrasting colour to show the pattern to the best advantage. Stuff well so that the crochet is slightly stretched.

DIAGRAM 56

Small doilies worked with narrow braids 15 mm ($\frac{1}{2}$ in) make attractive coasters. For an elegant table setting a linen luncheon mat with a hairpin edging could be teamed with a coaster. Edge the last round of the coaster to match the edging of the mat.

Diag 56 Hairpin motif coasters

OLD HAIRPIN DOILIES (from the author's private collection)

Examples of old hairpin work can be of great inspiration to the modern worker, who will not only marvel at the time spent creating such fine cobwebs, but will be provided with ideas for joins and edgings which can be adapted. Although such fine table linen is still a delight to use, these round work patterns can be translated into larger articles such as table or dressing-table mats, using a thicker cotton, or cushions made up of wider braids of wool.

All the following old doilies were made of cotton, but because crochet cottons have altered over the years some of these yarns no longer exist. The yarns described here can only be quoted as the nearest equivalent.

Fig 51–54 Views of 4 antique doilies

DOILY I 30 cm (12 in) DIAMETER (FIGURE 51)

This lovely doily worked in No. 60 cotton and has 5 rounds of 25 mm (1 in) basic braid. The loops are twisted except for the outer edge of the 4th round. All joins use the chevron method, but note how the last round of joins has been adapted to accommodate the fan braid. The whole is edged with 2 rows of crochet chain lace to give a picot effect (figure 51a).

74

DOILY 2 24 cm (9 in) DIAMETER (FIGURE 52)

This example features a linen damask centre with the well-favoured Victorian feather stitch embroidery around the edge. It has only 2 rounds of 20 mm ($\frac{3}{4}$ in) basic braid worked in No. 60 crochet cotton with a very distinct long chevron join. This variation of a chevron join is only successful in rounds. The broad band of crocheted Solomon's knot makes a pleasing design finished with groups of 3 picots (figure 52a).

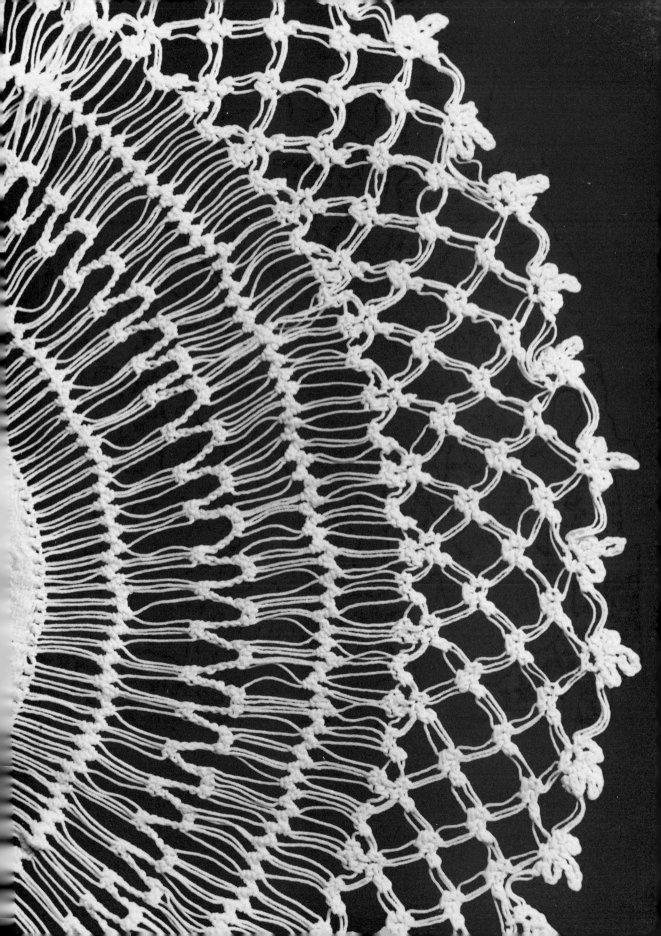

DOILY 3 24 cm (9 in) DIAMETER (FIGURE 53)

Another example of a linen centre having 3 rounds of 25 mm (1 in) basic braid worked in No. 10 crochet cotton. The loops are all twisted into the chevron join, the edging being a frivolous round of picots worked into every single loop (figure 53a).

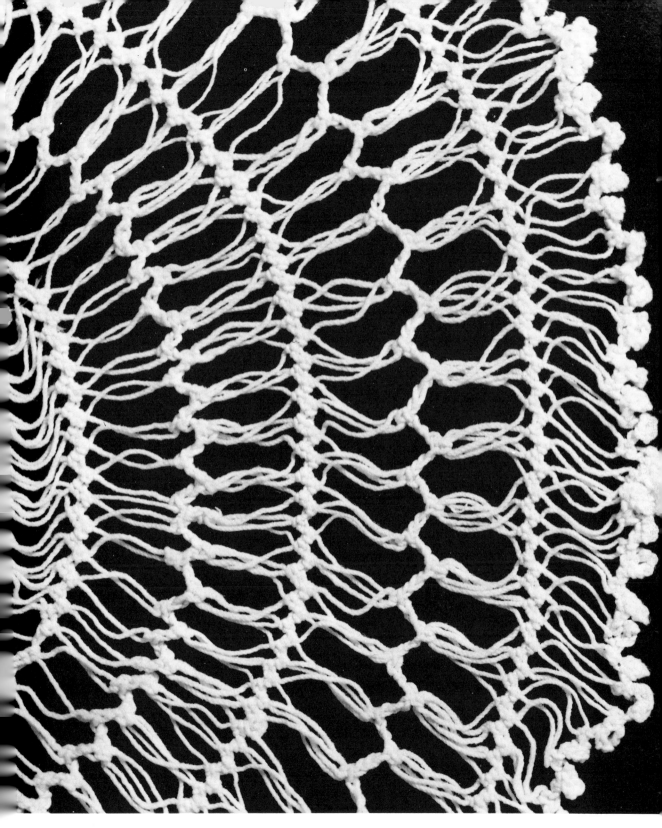

DOILY 4 24 cm (9 in) DIAMETER (FIGURE 54)

This very fragile doily is worked in sewing cotton on a wide 40 mm (1½ in) hairpin with only 2 rounds of braid. The central motif is chain lace crochet. The chevron join forms the fans which produces the wavy edging emphasised by the band of chain lace.

Lovely to look at, but not at all practical in use.

10
MAKING A TRIANGULAR SHAPE

Shaping a hairpin fabric by increasing or de-creasing is a simple process which again occurs whilst working the headings. These simple garments are based on a triangle and therefore need gradual shaping on two sides. This is done by decreasing at both ends of each braid, joining 2 groups of loops on the 1st braid to 1 group of loops on the 2nd braid.

Fig 55 A triangular shawl

SHAWL

Measurements
140 × 80 cm (56 × 32 in) (figure 55, diagram 57). This shawl is made up of 17 horizontal lengths of braid. The 1st braid is the longest, having 140 lps which are taken up in groups of 4. Each braid is decreased by 8 lps, i.e. 4 at each end, so that the length of each successive braid is reduced by 8 lps.

Fig 55a A close-up of the shawl fabric

Details

100 g (4 oz) of 4 ply yarn for the braid. 50 g (2 oz) of 3 ply yarn for the joins. 4.00 mm (G6) crochet hook, 2.00 mm (B1) crochet hook, 50 mm (2 in) hairpin. The basic braid was used with join No. 7.

Method

1 1st braid: Work 140 lps. Finish off.

2 Using the 3 ply yarn work down 1 side as follows: 1 dc (sc) into a grp of 4 untwisted lps, 9 ch, 1 dc (sc) into the spine, 9 ch. Repeat to the end (35 grps).

3 To decrease on the 2nd side: 1 dc (sc) into the 1st grp of 4 lps, 1 dc (sc) into the 2nd grp of 4 lps (decrease made) (diagram 58). *9 ch, 1 dc (sc) into the spine, 9 ch, 1 dc (sc) into a grp of 4 lps. Repeat from * to the last 8 lps. 1 dc (sc) into a grp of 4 lps twice. Fasten off. 1 grp of 4 lps have now been decreased at each end.

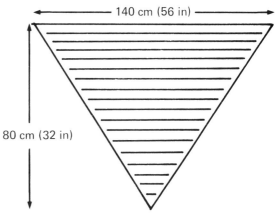

Diag 57 Diagram for a triangular shawl

4 2nd braid: Work 132 lps.

5 Using the 3 ply yarn join to the 1st braid as follows: 1 dc (sc) into the 1st grp of 4 lps, 1 sl st between the 2 dc (sc) of the decrease on the 1st braid (diagram 59). *9 ch, 1 dc (sc) into the spine of the 2nd braid, 9 ch, 1

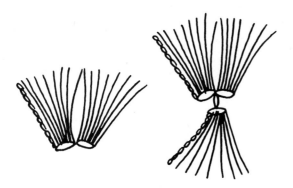

Diag 58 Decreasing groups of loops (1st braid)
Diag 59 Joining on the 2nd braid

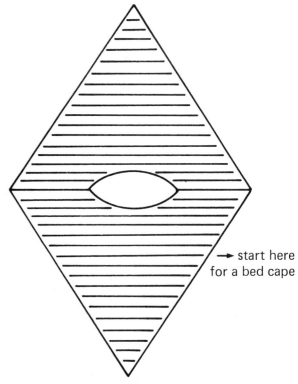

→ start here
for a bed cape

Diag 60 Diagram for a poncho

dc (sc) into the next grp of 4 lps, 1 sl st into the next grp on the 1st braid. Repeat from * to the last 4 lps which are joined with 1 sl st between the 2 dc (sc) on the 1st briad.

6 2nd side: Decrease as given for the 1st braid.

7 3rd braid: Work 124 lps.

8 Join and decrease as for the 2nd braid. Continue in this manner until 12 lps remain.

9 Final decrease: 1 dc (sc) into each of 3 grps.

10 Fringe: Cut 20 cm (8 in) lengths of 4 ply yarn, knot 3 lengths together into the 2 decreased edges.

VARIATIONS USING THE TRIANGULAR SHAPE

PONCHO WORKED TO THE SHAWL SIZE (DIAGRAM 60)

This is made with 2 triangles joined at the shoulder, but leaving a neck opening.

Method
1 1st side: Complete as for the shawl.

2 2nd side: Work in the same way, but do not work the top heading on the 1st length.

3 Join: Work the top heading of the 2nd side also joining each grp to its counterpart on the 1st side until 13 grps have been joined. Work the heading only across 9 grps for the neck opening. Head and join the 13 remaining grps.

4 Neck edge: Work a substantial heading with 2 rows of dc (sc). Make sure the crochet does not tighten the opening.

BED CAPE OR A CHILD'S PONCHO 92 × 60 cm (36 × 24 in) (DIAGRAM 60)

Adapt the poncho pattern to a smaller size by starting about $\frac{1}{3}$ of the way down using 11 braids.

Method
1st braid: Work 92 lps, take up into 23 grps. Work and finish as for the poncho.

USING DIFFERENT YARNS

If a thicker yarn is preferred, work the 1st length of braid to match the finished measurement given with the pattern. This will need less loops and must be a multiple of 4.

84

III

CREATIVE
HAIRPIN
CROCHET

11
COMBINING TECHNIQUES

The worker having now become familiar with the many techniques of hairpin crochet, this section shows how these may be combined to make attractive items, some useful, others for fun. Complete instructions are given to give the worker experience and confidence. For the adventurous the patterns can be adapted for a completely individual result.

COMBINING DIFFERENT WIDTHS OF BRAID

By the simple means of using two different widths of braid interesting stripe patterns can be designed. This cushion cover shows the use of alternating wide and narrow braids with the 2 colours intermingling in the cable join. The loops of the narrow braid are taken up completely, which in this instance adds to the success of the design. Other possibilities could be two wide braids alternated with one narrow braid or vice versa.

CUSHION COVER MEASURING 40 × 32 cm (16 × 13 in) (FIGURE 56)

The cover is worked in one piece and folded crosswise. The side edges are joined and fringed and a zip is used to close the bottom edge.

Details
Double knitting crepe yarn 80 g (4 oz) of a dark colour, 40 g (2 oz) of a light colour. 4.00 mm (G6) crochet hook, 80 mm (3 in) and 40 mm (1½ in) hairpins. 35 cm (14 in) zip fastener. The narrow braid is worked in basic braid. The wide braid is worked in No. 1 braid. Joining by 2-2 cable.

Method
1 Main piece: Work 5 dark lengths of the wide braid having 84 lps. Work 6 light lengths of the narrow braid also having 84 lps.

2 Join together alternately with the 2-2 cable (figure 56a). Refer to Chapter 6 figure 38 to give a well-shaped fabric.

3 Gusset join: Work 2 dark lengths of narrow braid for the side gussets having 42 lps. Fold the main piece in half crosswise. Using the cable join, insert the gussets by cabling one side to the cushion front and the other side to the cushion back.

4 Opening edges: Spacing evenly, work 9 dc (sc) into the wide braid and 6 dc (sc) into the narrow braid. Work 2 rows of dc (sc).

5 Insert the zip using a back stitch in matching wool.

6 Fringe: Fold the gusset braid double lengthways and work 1 row of dc (sc) into the spine along its length.

7 Cut 15 cm (6 in) lengths of dark yarn. Knot 3 lengths into each alternate dc (sc).

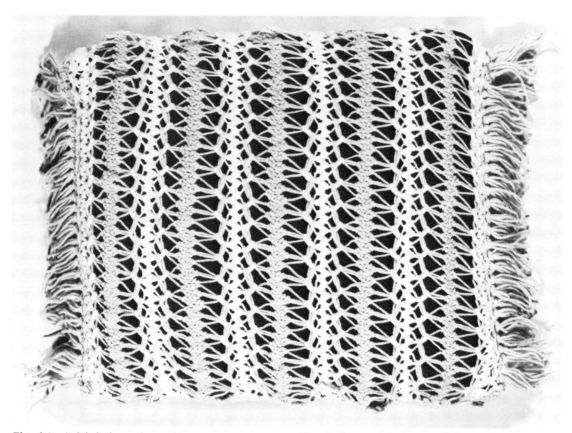

Fig 56 (top) A hairpin crochet cushion cover

Fig 56a (bottom) A close-up of the cushion fabric

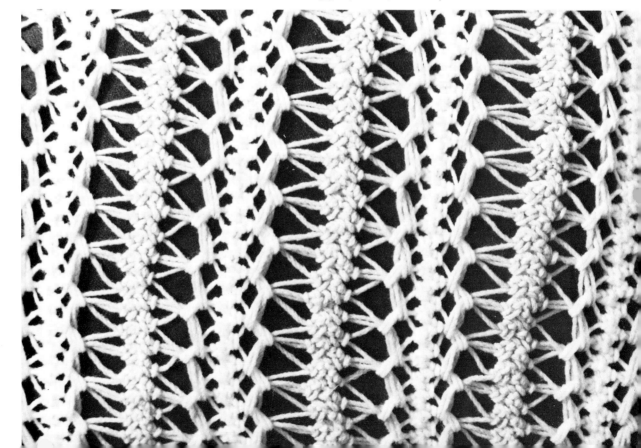

8 Line the cushion with a suitable colour to enhance the crochet.

COMBINING BRAID AND RIBBON

Inserting hairpin braid between lengths of ribbon produces a very pleasing contrast between solid fabric and lacy braid. The evening bag shows a simple interpretation of this idea.

EVENING BAG MEASURING 20 × 11 cm (8 × 4½ in) (FIGURE 57)

Details

1 ball of perle cotton 3, or fine craft yarn, or lurex yarn. 2.50 mm (C2) crochet hook. 20 mm (¾ in) hairpin. 1.5 m (1½ yd) of 20 mm (¾ in) wide velvet ribbon. 2 pieces of lining fabric 20 × 30 cm (8 × 12 in). Sequins optional. Basic braid with a plain heading (braid 8, figure 11).

Method

1 Work 5 lengths of braid 27 cm (11 in) long, approximately 46 lps.

2 Work the headings, 1 dc (sc), 1 ch, along each side.

3 Insert the braids between four 30 cm (12 in) lengths of ribbon using fine oversewing, leaving 1 cm (½ in) ribbon at each end. Follow the same method of joining as explained for hairpin fabrics in Chapter 6 diagram 38, even though the braids are not joined to each other (figure 57a).

4 Turn back the raw edges of the ribbon and stitch in place.

5 Turn up 10 cm (4 in) to form the pocket leaving 75 cm (3 in) for the flap. Starting from the bottom corner, join the pocket edges together by working 1 dc (sc) through the outer headings. Continue up the side of the flap.

6 Along the flap edge work *1 dc (sc) into the 1st braid lp, 1 dc (sc) into the spine, 1 dc (sc) into the next braid lp, 4 ch (to bridge the ribbon). Repeat from * to the flap corner.

7 Continue the dc (sc) down the second side, finishing at the bottom corner.

8 For the handle make a ch 30 cm (12 in) long. Turn and work 1 dc (sc) into each ch. Stitch in place.

9 For the lining place both pieces, right sides together. Stitch 1.5 cm (½ in) from the edge leaving an opening.

10 Turn right sides out and stitch the opening.

11 Turn up 10 cm (4 in) to form the pocket and oversew together.

12 Place inside the bag and catch stitch in position. Close the flap with 2 snap fasteners.

13 If desired sew sequins on to the flap ribbons.

Variations

1 Use braids and ribbons of differing widths, e.g. taffeta combined with one of the more intricate insertions.

2 Webbing combined with string braids for a casual pochette.

3 Use braid insertions between solid bands of plain crochet.

COMBINING JOINS

The use of two different joins in the construction of a fabric will add further interest, for example cable joins produce a broad, dense band which can be contrasted with an openwork join. In the bag illustrated a cable join was used with a double crochet (sc) join for a rich textural quality. Two widths of hairpins were also used for practical as well as aesthetic reasons – to avoid making the double crochet (sc) too spidery.

SHOPPING BAG MEASURING 40 × 33 cm (16 × 13 in) (FIGURE 58)

Details

100 g (4 oz) thick dishcloth yarn, craft yarn or nylon yarn. 4.50 mm (7) crochet hook. 50 mm (2 in) and 25 mm (1 in) hairpins. ½ m (½ yd) of canvas (burlap) 90 cm (36 in) wide. Basic braid. Joins: Double crochet (sc) and 2 to 2 cable.

Fig 57 An evening bag using hairpin insertions

Fig 57a A close-up of the evening bag fabric

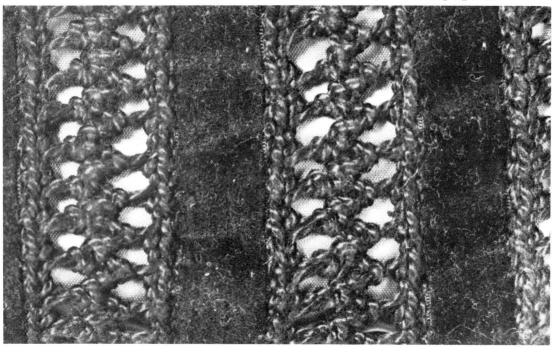

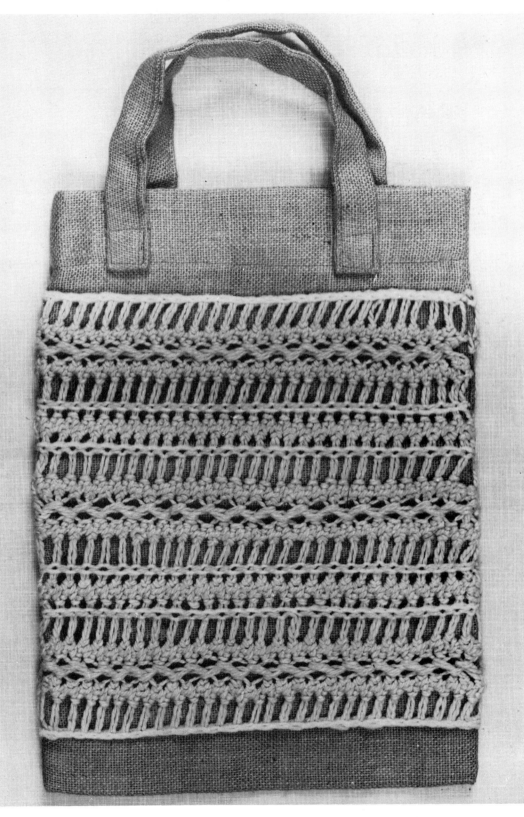

Method

1 For each panel work 6 lengths of wide braid with 30 lps or 35 cm (14 in) long.

2 Join the wide braids together in pairs with 2 to 2 cabling.

3 Work 2 lengths of narrow braid with 30 lps or 35 cm (14 in) long.

4 Join in the narrow braids between the cabled braids with dc (sc) join.

5 Along the top and bottom edges work 1 dc (sc) into each lp.

6 With right side facing, work a sl st into each dc (sc).

7 Damp well, pin to shape on a board and allow to dry.

Fig 58 A shopping bag with decorative hairpin panels
Fig 58a Close-ups of the hairpin panel

To make the canvas bag (diagram 61)

1 For the main part cut a piece 90 × 35 cm (36 × 14 in).

2 For the handles cut the remaining strip into 2 to give 2 pieces 45 × 10 cm (18 × 4 in).

3 Apply the 2 hairpin panels 13 cm (5 in) from each end, stitch all the way round.

4 Fold the bag across the middle, right sides together. Check that the hairpin bands match at the side edges. Machine stitch the sides together. Bind or overcast the raw edges.

5 Turn in the top edge 5 cm (2 in) and stitch.

6 To make the handles, turn in the long edges 2.5 cm (1 in) and press. Fold in half lengthways to give a 2.5 cm (1 in) wide strip. Press and stitch close to the edge.

7 Turn up the raw ends 2.5 cm (1 in) and stitch in place securely.

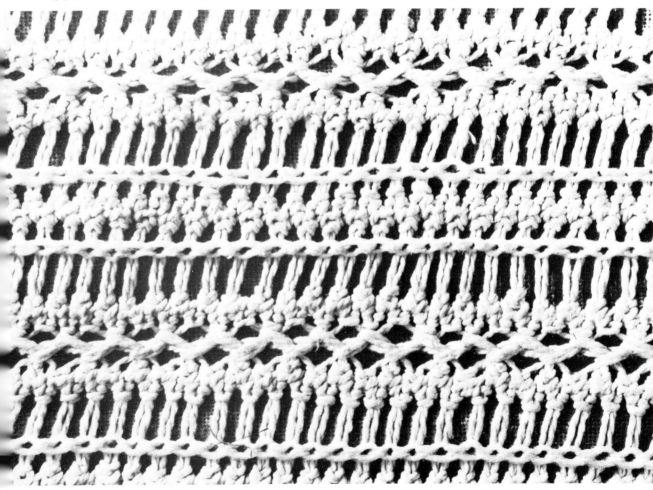

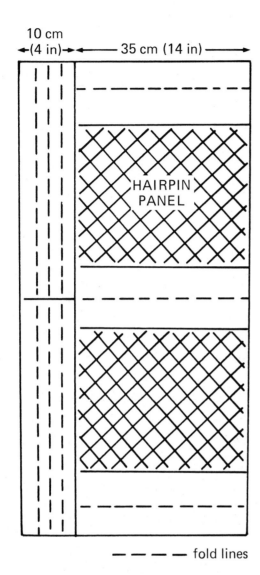

10 cm
◄─(4 in)─►◄─── 35 cm (14 in) ───►

HAIRPIN
PANEL

─ ─ ─ ─ ─ fold lines

Diag 61 Diagram for a shopping bag with a hairpin fabric panel

COMBINING TEXTURES

Hairpin lace fabrics present a natural opportunity to combine contrasting textures. Sometimes it is more practicable to use a finer thread for the join, especially when a bulkier yarn is used for the braid, but here is a chance to combine thick and thin, rough and smooth,

fluffy and silky to give a fresh dimension to the work. For laundering purposes it is safer to avoid mixing natural with man-made fibres.

KIMONO JACKET (FIGURE 59)

This basic design is adaptable to many uses depending upon the character of the chosen yarns.

Details

1.75 g (7 oz) of a light, bulky acrylic for the braids. 50 g (2 oz) of 3 ply glossy acrylic for the joins. 5.00 mm (H8) and 2.50 mm (C2) crochet hooks. 60 mm ($2\frac{1}{2}$ in) hairpin. Braid No. 3. Join 2, chevron style (Chapter 6).

Measurements

To fit 85–95 cm (34–38 in) bust. For larger sizes use a 80 mm (3 in) hairpin. Length from shoulder to lower edge 46 cm (18 in).

Method (diagram 62)

1 Bodice: Work 6 lengths with 84 lps (90 cm (36 in) long).

2 Work 1 length with 40 lps (42 cm (17 in) long) for the centre back.

3 For the join work a plain heading of 1 dc (sc), 3 ch into each lp on both sides of each braid.

4 Join together as shown in diagram 62 by working 1 dc (sc) 3 ch into the ch space of each braid alternately.

5 Sleeves: Work 6 lengths with 44 lps (46 cm (18 in) long) with the headings.

6 Miss 20 lps from the bottom edge of the bodice, then join on the sleeve braids as for the bodice.

7 To make up: Fold at the shoulder matching A to A, B to B and C to C. Join the bodice side seams A to B with the chevron join.

8 Knot together the sleeve edges B to C using the loose ends.

Edging (figure 59a): Using the thicker yarn work 2 rows of tr (dc) all round the edges of the bodice and sleeves as follows. On the front edges work 1 tr (dc) into each ch space. Along

Fig 59 A hairpin Kimono jacket
Fig 59a A close-up of the jacket fabric
Diag 62 Diagram for a kimono jacket

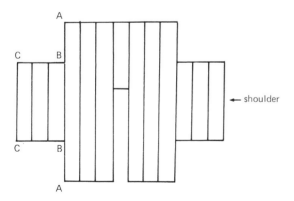

the lower edge work 3 tr (dc) into each lp, 1 tr (dc) into the spine of the braid, 1 tr (dc) into the chevron join.

At the corners work 3 tr (dc) into the same place. Using the fine yarn and a 5.00 mm (H8) hook work 1 row of sl st into the 2nd row of trebles.

VARIATIONS

Diagram 63

The kimono design can be adapted to make a longer jacket by making bodice braids of approximately 100 loops. The sleeves can be lengthened by adding more braids.

Diag 64 A blouson jacket

Method (diagram 65)

1 Make 4 braids with 84 lps for the main bodice, 1 braid with 40 lps for the centre back, 2 braids with 20 lps for the under arm.

2 Join together as shown in diagram 65 using the chevron join.

3 Fold at the shoulder matching A to A and B to B. Join from A to B.

4 Work the edgings as for the kimono jacket.

Diag 63 A long hairpin fabric jacket

Diagram 64

For a blouson effect the loops along the lower edge can be gathered into a deep crochet edging by working only 2 tr (dc) into each loop at the waist. Fasten with a button or add ties.

Waistcoat

This is worked on the same principle, but with the addition of a short length of braid at the sides for underarm shaping. Follow the details given for the kimono jacket.

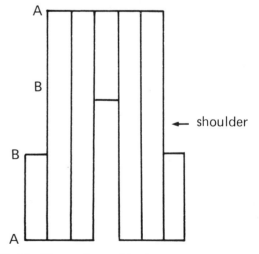

Diag 65 Diagram for a waistcoat

94

12
BRAID LACES

Braid or tape has long been used in the making of some forms of lace. Specially made braid was fashioned into elaborate designs for needle-made, bobbin and crochet laces. Because it is easy to manipulate, hairpin braid is ideal for this purpose and has many possibilities ranging from simple appliqué on a net ground to elaborate floral forms filled with a variety of crochet stitches.

APPLIQUÉ BRAID LACE

This is a simple method but it can be very effective. The techniques – that is, the use of decorative braids and appliqué motifs, methods which by now seem elementary – have been covered in previous chapters. The only difference is the base material, which is now a sheer fabric. The old laces of this type were worked on very fine, cotton muslin. Organdie is a very good substitute when available, otherwise choose a fine synthetic glass curtaining.

OVAL TRAY MAT MEASURING 27 × 19 cm (11 × 8 in), FIGURE 60

The narrow hairpin braid is used for the outer edging and the inner border. The basic motifs are made in 2 sizes.

Details
1 ball No. 60 crochet cotton. 0.75 mm (Steel 12) crochet hook. 10 mm ($\frac{1}{2}$ in) and 20 mm ($\frac{3}{4}$ in) hairpins. 0.25 m ($\frac{1}{4}$ yd) sheer material. Basic braid is used throughout.

To obtain the pattern: Diagram 66 shows half the full size shape. Fold a double size piece of tracing paper in half, crease and open out. Place the crease on the fold line indicated on the diagram. Trace the half shape boldly. Refold the tracing paper to draw the 2nd half.

Method
1 Pin the fabric over the paper pattern and trace the designs lighly in pencil.

2 Work 3 large motifs 20 mm ($\frac{3}{4}$ in) wide having 16 lps and 5 small motifs 10 mm ($\frac{1}{2}$ in) wide.

3 Arrange in a pleasing manner or as shown in figure 60. Stitch in position, firstly in the centre, then round the lps with tiny stitches and fine sewing thread.

4 Work the narrow, inner border having approximately 180 lps.

5 Pin and tack in position. The inner lps are caught down with a chain stitch (embroidered) running parallel with the spine. The outer lps are caught down with small stitches.

6 The narrow outer braid requires approximately 280 lps.

7 Pin and tack in position, turning the braid over to negotiate the sharp scallop angles

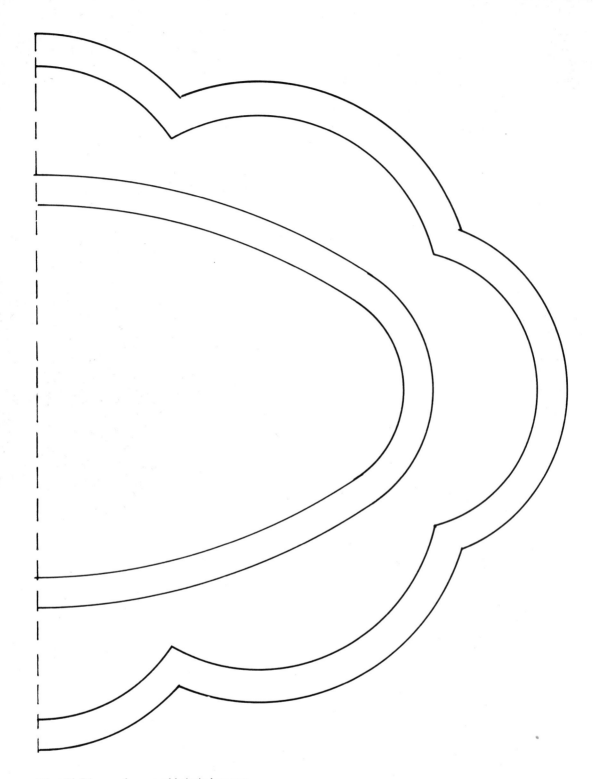

Diag 66 Diagram for an oval hairpin lace mat

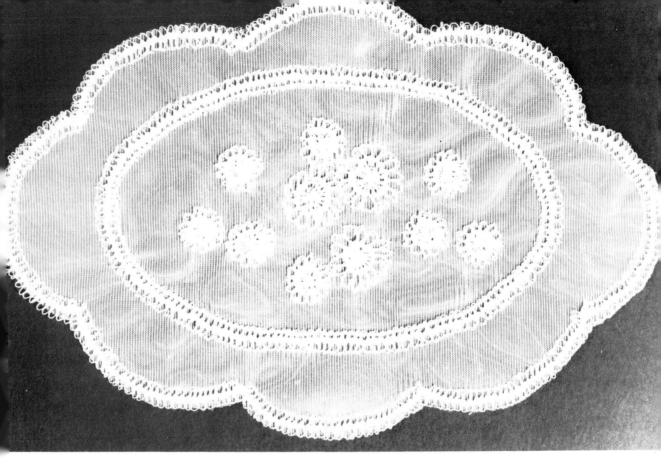

Fig 60 Oval tray mat with hairpin braid appliqué

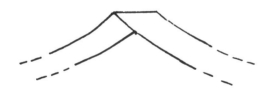

Diag 67 Turning the appliqué braid

(diagram 67). Use small stitches to catch down the inner lps, the outer lps are left free.

8 Cut away the spare fabric to just outside the scallop edging. Turn back and stitch down on to the spine.

RENAISSANCE BRAID LACE

This is a needle-made lace where the braid design is held by embroidery stitches. This example uses a simple form of Teneriffe lace method where threads are laid across the spaces and held by needle weaving. Button-holed bars, faggoting and herring-bone stitch may also be used.

ROUND MAT MEASURING 15 cm (6 in) DIAMETER (FIGURE 61)

Apart from the small centre ring the braid is worked in one continuous length. The braid is tacked on to the paper pattern ready for the stitchery.

Details

1 ball of No. 5 perle cotton for the braid. 1 ball of No. 8 perle cotton for the stitchery. 1.50 mm (Steel 7) crochet hook. 15 mm ($\frac{1}{2}$ in) hairpin. Basic braid. To obtain the pattern trace diagram 68 and transfer to stout wrapping paper using dressmakers' tracing paper.

Method

1 Work a basic braid with 16 lps. Join into a ring and fasten off.

2 Tack in place on the pattern.

97

3 Work a basic braid 125 cm (50 in) long. Tack in position keeping the braid flat.

4 Stitch the intersections with small, firm stitches. Running a sewing thread through the spine, stitch the lps together where shown on the diagram.

5 Work webs into the spaces as follows:

To work the stitchery
1 Following the numbers, lay threads across the space running the needle through the spine (diagram 69).

Fig 61 Reniassance braid lace mat

2 Take the thread to the centre by whipping over 1 spoke (diagram 70).

3 Weave the thread under and over the centre spokes in spiral fashion (diagram 71).

4 Whip each remaining spoke by working out from the centre, running through the spine to the adjoining spoke and whipping back to the centre again (diagram 72).

Adjust the spokes for the triangular spaces. Finally, cut the tacking threads at the back of the paper to release the finished lace.

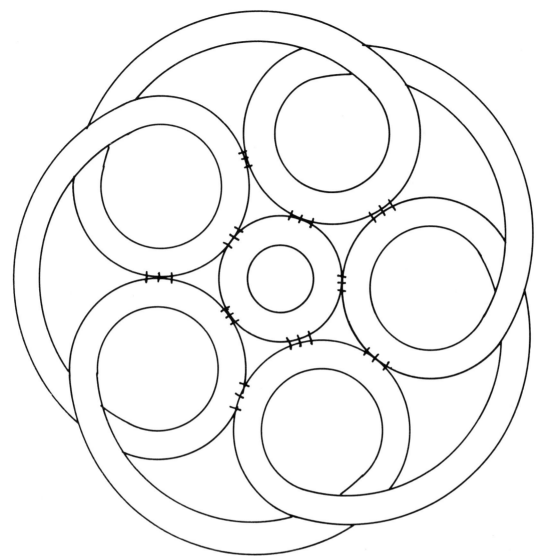

Diag 68 Diagram for a Renaissance braid mat

Diag 69–72 Stages in working the stitchery

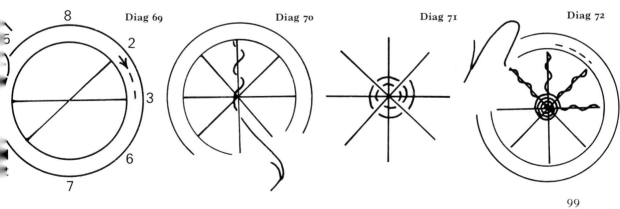

CROCHET BRAID LACE

The scroll design in this example is held in place by crochet chains and floral motifs. This can be seen as a development of the joining method instead of filling a straight strip the crochet must be varied to fill irregular spaces.

SCROLL LACE 6 cm (2½ in) WIDE (FIGURE 62)

Details

No. 40 crochet cotton. 1.00 mm (Steel 10) crochet hook. 10 mm (½ in) hairpin. Basic braid. Each scroll has 44 lps and measures 2.5 cm (1 in).

Method

Work sufficient basic braid for desired length (multiples of 44 loops plus 22 to finish the last scroll).

1 dc (sc) into first lp, 6 ch. Miss 2 lps, 1 dc (sc) into next lp, 6 ch. Miss 2 lps, 1 dc (sc) into next lp. 14 ch, sl st into 6th ch from hook to form a ring (centre of flower motif), 6 ch. Miss 3 lps, dc (sc) into next group of 2 lps.

Work back along the last 6 ch to form the first petal as follows: 1 dc (sc), 4 tr (dc) into ring, 6 ch. Miss 3 lps, 1 dc (sc) into next grp of 2 lps.

Work back along 6 ch as before, 1 dc (sc) into ring, 6 ch. Miss 3 lps, 1 dc (sc) into next lp. Work a petal, 6 ch. Miss 3 lps, 1 dc (sc) into next grp of 2 lps, work petal, 6 ch. Miss 3 lps, 1 dc (sc) into next grp of 2 lps, work petal.

For the 6th petal work along the long chain at the top of the flowers 4 tr (dc), 1 dc (sc). 3 ch. Miss 3 lps, 1 dc (sc) into next lp, 3 ch. 1 dc (sc) into middle of opposite ch, 3 ch. Miss 2 lps, 1 dc (sc) into next lp, 3 ch. 1 dc (sc) into middle of opposite ch, 3 ch. Miss 2 lps, 1 dc (sc) into next lp. Fasten off.

For the second scroll commence in the loop opposite the 4th petal.

TO WORK VARIATIONS

Ingenious needle-workers can work out their own variations by drawing a design for the braid on to a piece of firm material, e.g. cotton sheeting. The probable positions of the joining stitches are also marked and then the braid is tacked in position. The crochet joins can then be worked to the crocheter's own discretion.

Fig 62 Crochet scroll lace. The width of each motif is 2.5 cm (1 in) and the whole pattern measures 6 cm (2½ in) from top to bottom

13
HOW TO CREATE AND EXPERIMENT

As printed patterns for hairpin crochet can be difficult to find, it is useful and satisfying to design one's own. Contrary to some beliefs, it is not essential to sit before a blank piece of paper and draw a finished article, in fact there is no need to draw at all. Start with the germ of an idea, follow the step-by-step instructions, be prepared to spend some time experimenting and let the idea grow. If the reader has worked through this book, especially Parts I and II, it will be realised that some of the hints given here have been covered earlier when the need arose. They are now brought together with additional information to form a set of guide lines to help the worker organise equipment, materials, measurements and ideas. It is quite likely that a completed project could be the base for further pieces using the same theme. To quote the old adage, 'One thing leads to another'.

PREPARATIONS

Well-planned preparations will lay a good foundation for the real business of creative work and will avoid starting with a confused jumble of equipment and yarns which in turn leads to a jumble of ideas.

EQUIPMENT

Try to build up a wide range of hairpins and materials.

Crochet hooks
Most workers will have already acquired at least one hook from each of the fine, medium and large categories e.g. 1.50 mm (7), 4.00 mm (G6) and 6.00 mm (J10). Consult the hook size tables at the beginning of this book, which show the range of hooks available. Gradually fill in the gaps according to personal requirements. Obviously a person who prefers working with thicker yarns will concentrate on collecting wool hooks first.

Hairpins
The hairpin loom described in chapter 1 diagram 3 is a valuable aid for experimenting. The addition of hairpins 15 mm ($\frac{1}{2}$ in), 20 mm ($\frac{3}{4}$ in), 25 mm (1 in) and 40 mm ($1\frac{1}{2}$ in) will make a good basic set.

Arrange hooks and hairpins in order of size in purchased cases or home-made wallets so they can be easily selected.

Other items
Paper, pencils, pins, small ruler for measuring tension, tape measure.

YARNS

Many workers will have accumulated oddments of knitting and crochet yarns; the greater the variety of thickness, texture and colour the better. Watch the wool shops for remnants of all types, find strings and twines in stationery departments and garden shops. Look for rug wools, finer carpet yarns, unfinished yarns at markets, browse around the craft suppliers for synthetic raffia and macramé cords or the haberdashery counters for Russian braid and very narrow ribbons. Match the yarns to the crochet hooks by putting a slip loop into the hook where it should fit easily.

SAMPLES

It cannot be emphasised too much that the working of the samples given in Parts I and II of this book will be a valuable experience. These can be mounted in scrap books or loose-leaf files, keeping each type together. Alternately, secure the samples on a roll of substantial fabric so that it can be rolled up scroll fashion. When working, this can be unrolled to show a spread of as many samples as required.

Assemble all equipment and yarns before starting.

STARTING A DESIGN

COLLECTING IDEAS

Most readers will have already made several kinds of braids and fabrics and in some way will have altered them to suit their own taste. This is a first step to design. For inspiration look again at the 'suggested uses' passages in Parts I and II of this book and try to visualise how these could be elaborated or altered. Further ideas can be gleaned from many sources. Look in needlework books, in libraries and museums, magazines and fashion pages, and shop windows. You will not find hairpin crochet, but you can consider how it could replace other forms of decoration.

DEVELOPING IDEAS FOR BRAIDS

The most important factor is purpose. Good design is always based on efficiency, and this should be kept in mind throughout each stage. Have the chosen article, now called the background, to hand so that the hairpin braid can grow on it. Assemble the equipment and as many yarns as possible and now forget the word 'design' and substitute 'choose', keeping in mind the purpose of the article you are working on.

1. Width
Choose the width of the finished braid. Cut lengths of paper to the estimated width and pin to the background. Does it look right? Is it well placed? Experiment with different widths and positions until it satisfies. Make a note of the width and position.

2. Yarn
Choose a yarn of suitable thickness and texture. Do not worry about colour at this stage. If the article is to be laundered, all yarns must be washable and colour fast. Beware of mixing natural and synthetic yarns and background fabrics in case of shrinkage, or test them before making up. Look at the yarn against the background.

3. Braid style
Choose a suitable braid pattern by referring to the samples. Take into consideration twisted loops and groups of loops which will initially need a wider foundation braid and decide whether a heading will be used.

With these factors in mind, select the correct hairpin and with the chosen yarn make a sample with 12 loops. Does it look right against the background? If not, try an alternative.

4. Headings
Choose a heading (if used), again referring to the samples.

Choose a yarn. This can be the yarn used for the braid or a finer yarn of different texture. Work the chosen heading on to the foundation braid. Test the result against the background.

5. Colour
Choose a colour or a colour scheme. This is a very personal choice, but if in doubt use shades of one colour including that of the background; or pile a selection of colours on to the background, then add or subtract colours until there is a harmonious result.

Choose the braid colour first, as this will be

dominant. Lay strands against the background in roughly the same proportion as the braid and headings, experimenting until the balance looks right.

If it is necessary, purchase new yarns in the correct thickness and colour and make a final sample. Study the result with a critical eye. Leave it on the background in a prominent position so that it can be judged with a fresh eye.

TO COMPLETE THE BRAID

The design is now complete. Using the finished sample, estimate the number of loops needed for the finished work. Gauge the number of loops within 2.5 cm (1 in) as described in chapter 5, diagram 28. Finally attach the braid to its appointed position, using the most suitable method shown in Chapter 3.

KEEPING A RECORD

Keep the samples, together with a written record of the following facts: braid width and pattern, heading pattern, yarns, tension and tools. These facts may be useful for future projects and it could save time not having to gauge and measure.

DEVEOPING IDEAS FOR FABRICS

The same rule applies to hairpin fabrics, namely, the result must be suitable to its purpose.

1. Planning
Make a plan of the size and shape on paper.

2. Yarns
Choose a yarn that is in character with the project. Look in the oddments bag first.

3. Braids
Choose a braid width, depending upon the thickness of the yarn, the laciness of the proposed fabric and the taking up of the loops for the joins. If a cable join is envisaged this must be given special consideration. Choose a braid pattern. Make 2 sample lengths of about 20 loops.

4. Join
Choose a join and a suitable yarn and test it on the 2 sample braids. Decide whether the braids will run vertically or horizontally.

5. Estimating
Measure the width of one braid and one join and compare this with the planned size of the finished fabric.

To adjust, alter either the braid width or the join or both. Remember there will be a braid on both edgings, so calculate the number of braids and joins plus 1 extra braid. Gauge the number of loops as explained for braid designs.

6. Yarn estimates
If a large amount of yarn will be needed, purchase 1 ball for the braid and work a complete length. It may be possible to judge how much yarn has been used; or, if possible, use a sensitive weighing scale to calculate the amount required. The join will not need very much, but the amount can be assessed when a few joins have been made.

To complete
Work a suitable edging to finish (Chapter 6).

Keep a record of the sample and details regarding tools, braid, widths, joins and tension.

14

HAIRPIN EDGINGS USING A DIFFERENT TECHNIQUE

This collection of edgings is worked in a completely different way, in that the loops are formed by passing the yarn round the left prong. Double crocheting (sc) is worked up the inner side of the prong, but in this case the turning of the pin does not form the loops, it simply transfers the working to the opposite prong. Because the crochet stitches are worked against the prong the loops are much smaller than the basic braid. To emphasise the dainty quality of these edgings they should be worked in fine yarn on a hairpin as narrow as possible.

Fig 63 No. 1 edging – work in progress

WORKING THE EDGING

The samples are worked in No. 10 crochet cotton for clarity only. No. 40 cotton or finer are much more suitable. Hold the prong with the open end uppermost and work up the left prong throughout.

NO. 1 EDGING (FIGURE 63)

1 Cast on as for the basic braid. Manipulate the loop so that the knot is close to the left prong instead of in the centre (diagram 73).

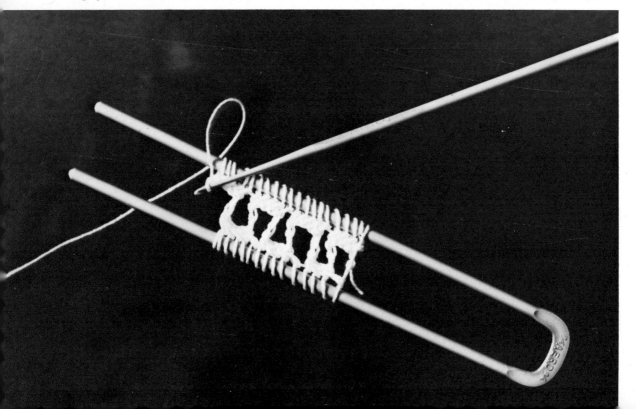

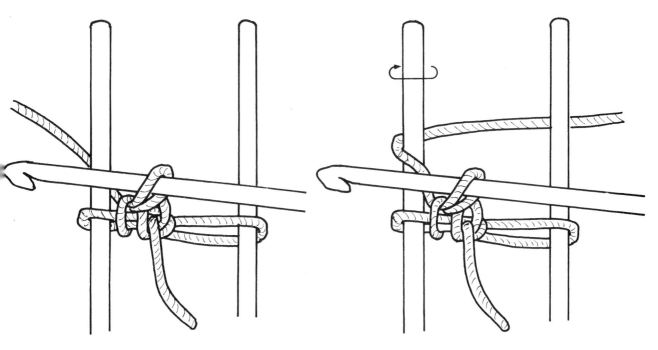

Diag 73 Hairpin edgings with a different technique

Diag 74–76 Working the stitches on the 1st side

2 Using the left hand, pass the yarn between the prongs, then in front of the left prong and round to the back as shown by the arrow (diagram 74).

3 Insert the hook into the front of the left loop; catch the yarn to work 1 dc (sc) (diagram 75).

4 Pass the yarn around the left prong, insert the hook into the front of the last lp, work 1 dc (sc) (diagram 76).

5 Repeat stage 4 until 5 dc (sc) have been worked up the left prong (this is a 5 dc (sc) group). Work 2 ch (diagram 77).

6 Turn the hairpin over from left to right so that the yarn lies across the empty prong.

7 Insert the hook into the front of the left (cast-on) loop and work 1 dc (sc) (diagram 78).

8 Repeat stages 4 to 6, having groups of 5 dc (sc) on each prong. When the hairpin is turned always remember to insert the hook into the last loop of the previous group.

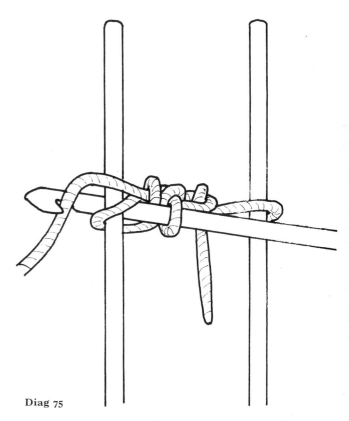

Diag 75

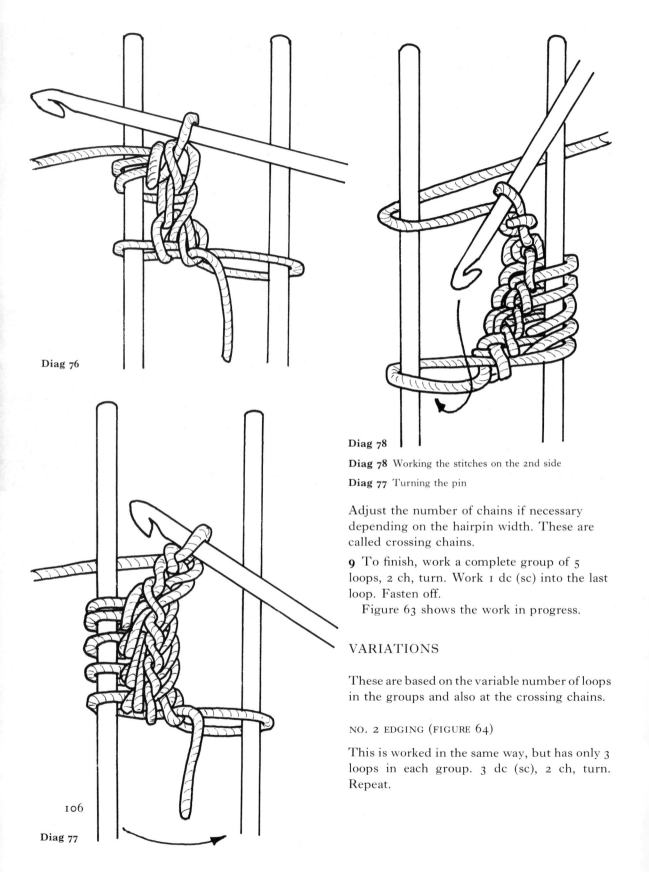

Diag 76

Diag 78

Diag 78 Working the stitches on the 2nd side

Diag 77 Turning the pin

Adjust the number of chains if necessary depending on the hairpin width. These are called crossing chains.

9 To finish, work a complete group of 5 loops, 2 ch, turn. Work 1 dc (sc) into the last loop. Fasten off.

Figure 63 shows the work in progress.

VARIATIONS

These are based on the variable number of loops in the groups and also at the crossing chains.

NO. 2 EDGING (FIGURE 64)

This is worked in the same way, but has only 3 loops in each group. 3 dc (sc), 2 ch, turn. Repeat.

Diag 77

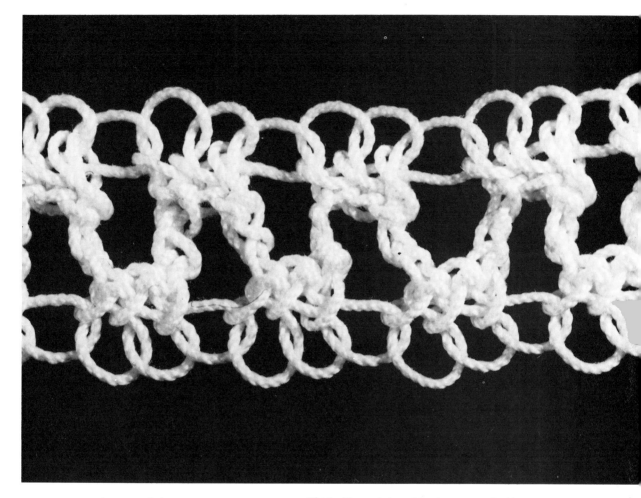

NO. 3 EDGING (FIGURE 65)

7 dc (sc), 2 ch, turn. Repeat.

NO. 4 EDGING (FIGURE 66)

This variation must be worked on a very fine pin as there are no crossing chains at all.

7 dc (sc), turn. Repeat. As before, the number of loops can be varied.

NO. 5 EDGING (FIGURE 67)

The number of loops on each side differ and there are no crossing chains. This edging is very quickly worked.

5 dc (sc), turn, 2 dc (sc), turn. Repeat.

NO. 6 EDGING (FIGURE 68)

Fig 64 No. 2 edging with 3 loops on each side

This is a variation of No. 3; the crossing chains are linked in the middle.

7 dc (sc), 5 ch, turn. 7 dc (sc), 2 ch, sl st into the 3rd of previous 5 ch, 2 ch turn. Repeat.

NO. 7 EDGING (FIGURE 69)

These pretty shells are formed when the hairpin is turned.

7 dc (sc), turn. 7 dc (sc), 1 sl st under the last crossing, turn.

FIGURE 70 SHOWS NO. 3 EDGING AROUND A HEART-SHAPED LAVENDAR BAG

No. 7 edging is used for the handkerchief.

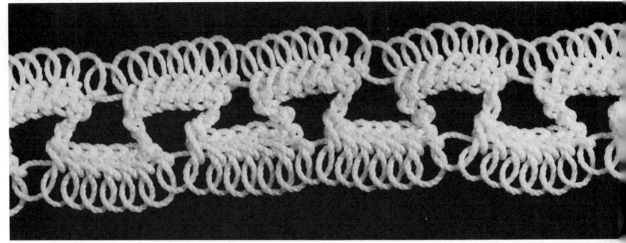

Fig 65 No. 3 edging with 7 loops on each side

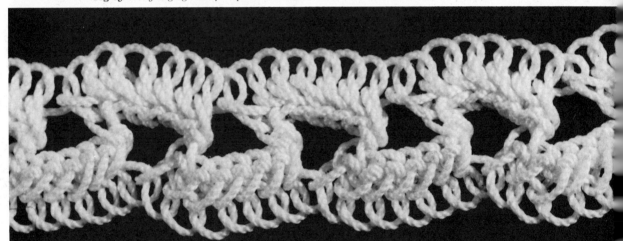

Fig 66 No. 4 edging – a fine edging without crossing chains

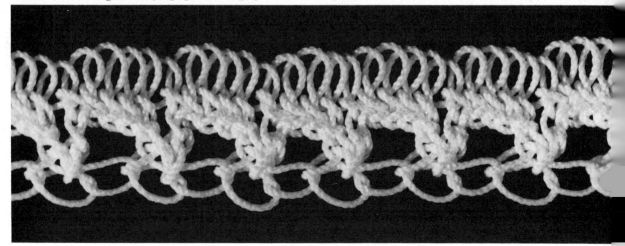

Fig 67 No. 5 edging with 5 loops on one side and 3 loops on the other

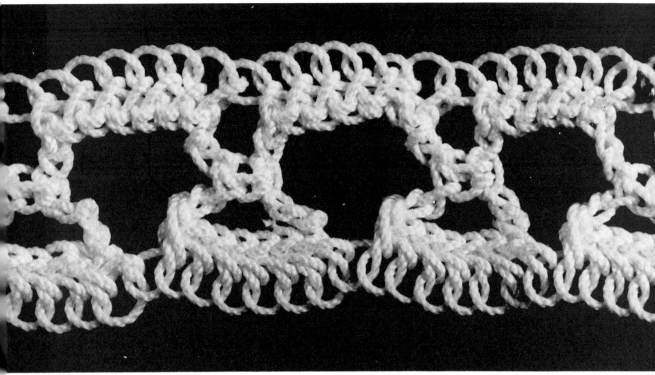

Fig 68 No. 6 edging with linked crossing chains

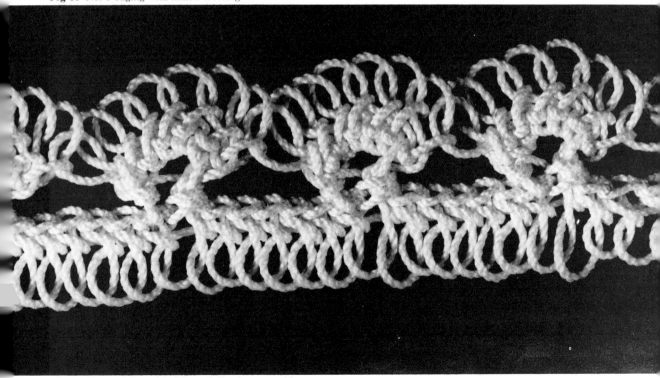

Fig 69 No. 7 edging with dainty shells along one side

Fig 70 A lavender bag and handkerchief edged with
hairpin edgings

15
HISTORICAL NOTES

THE DEVELOPMENT OF HAIRPIN CROCHET

Little is known about the origins of hairpin crochet, but it was not confined to the British Isles. Like many crafts it could have spread with population movement, for instance the trade routes from Europe to Asia carried exotic cargoes. Refugees, either political or religious, took with them the skills native to their homeland. The empire-builders who set up colonies in distant lands appointed all sorts of officials and their families. 'Fancy work' would help to pass away the long hours of an ocean voyage. So where hairpin work came from, or where it went, is just a matter of conjecture.

When hairpin work as at the height of its popularity in the latter part of the nineteenth century, patterns were available in ladies' journals and needlework magazines such as *Weldon's Practical Needlework*. Many ladies would not have access to them for financial reasons; others preferred to create their own patterns, often using home-made pins of wood, metal and bone. Ladies of leisure considered it a novel way of showing off their skills, so in this case the crochet crafts were mainly used for decorative purposes, and used with great enthusiasm. The less wealthy made it for more practical reasons. It was a quick, cheap and easy edging to use instead of lace, which was beyond their means. Many little girls' petticoats were trimmed in this way and many Sunday tea tables displayed a hairpin crochet doily.

Needlework groups were formed in many communities, often connected to the church or as classes run by patronising ladies for the betterment of the girls of the parish. All types of crochet samples were exchanged and copied, then mounted in scrap books made of brown paper or fabric. These skills, some of which were never written down, were handed down to the next generation.

Figure 71 shows various old samples of crochet braid lace. The purchased braid, previously mentioned in Chapter 12, can be identified by the pronounced loops which look very much like a hairpin braid. They are still mounted on the remains of a thick paper. Photograph by permission of the Trustees of the Rachel B. Kay Shuttleworth Collection.

During the Great War these little groups put away their fancy work to make comforters for the troops. This was to be the first step in the decline of crochet, including hairpin crochet. The remnants of its existence can be found tucked away in drawers among the treasured white table linen, the pride of a bygone housewife. Sadly it now goes unrecognised or is mistaken for another almost extinct craft – that of fine netting.

Figures 72 and 73 show one example of a hairpin doily and one of netting, which look very much alike. Study both close-up views and identify the spine and join on the first doily then try to find them on the 2nd doily.

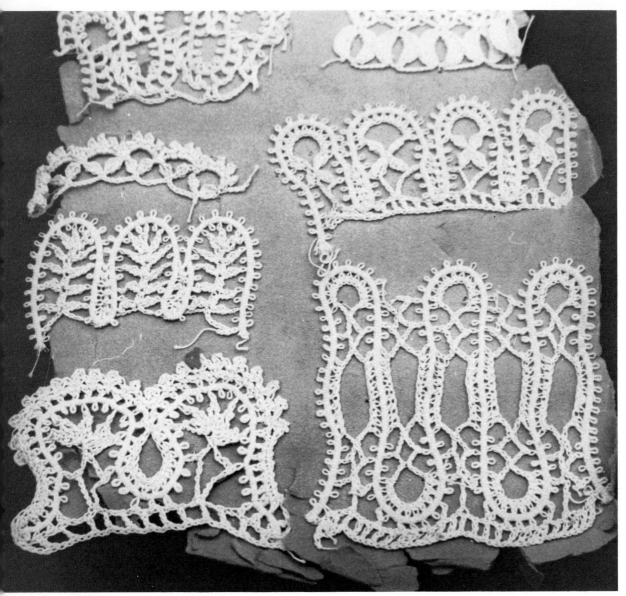

Fig 71 Samples of antique braid laces

Fig 72 An antique hairpin crochet doily
Fig 72a Close-up view

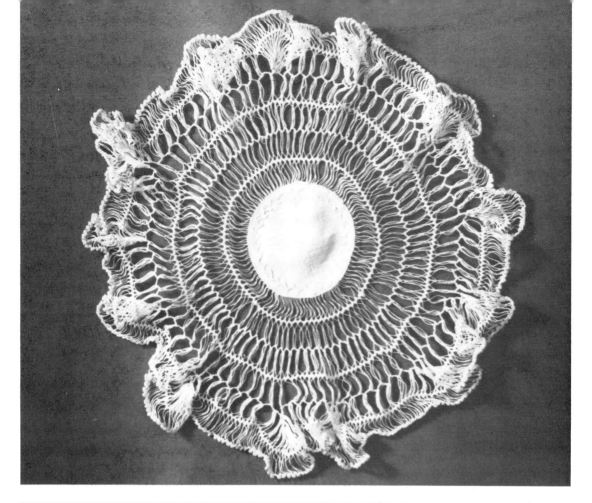

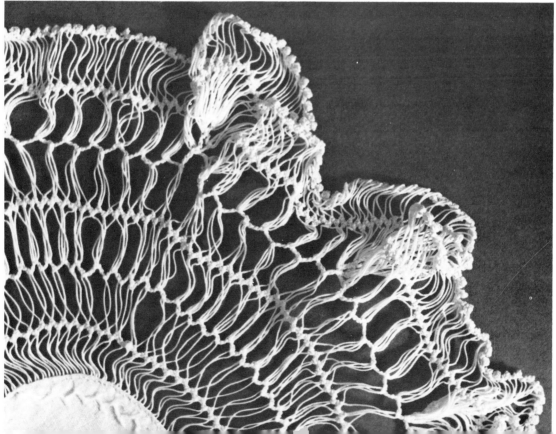

Fig 73 (top) An antique netted doily   **Fig 73a (bottom)** Close-up view

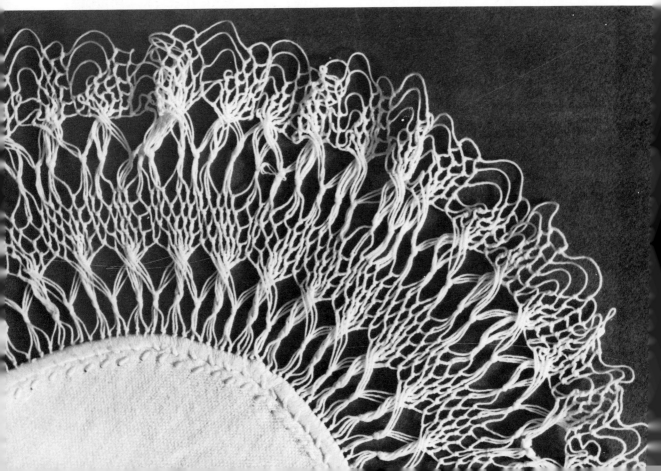

OLD TOOLS

During the Victorian era fringes were used
extensively in common with other forms of
embellishment. Hairpin crochet probably provided one of the quickest methods of producing
a fringe and so hairpins were made specially for
this purpose to ensure even working.

DIAGRAM 79

This type of hairpin was made to ensure that the
fringe was of even depth.

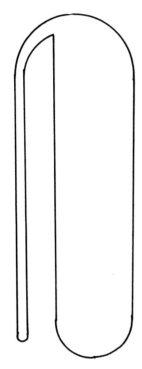

Diag 79 Old hairpins

DIAGRAM 80

This type of pin fulfils the same purpose, but
was made with extra prongs so that fringes
could be made with loops of different lengths.
For a zigzag fringe one loop was made round
each prong in succession following the
numbers.

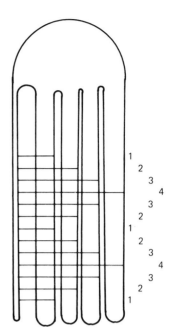

Diag 80 Hairpin for making a graduated fringe

DIAGRAM 81

This is another variation. The numbers show
how a two-tier fringe was made by alternating a
long loop with a short loop. For further embellishment tassels or pompoms were made and
attached to each loop.

Diag 81 Hairpin for making a 2-tiered fringe

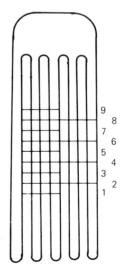

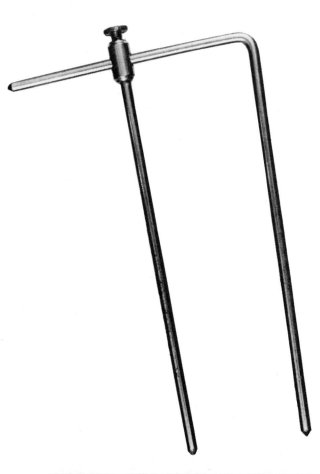

FIGURE 74

This tool is a forerunner of the modern adjustable loom. The right prong is movable along the top bar and can be adjusted to any width up to 7.5 cm (3 in). A screw is tightened to hold the prong in place. It is very heavy to use, as the manufacturers did not have the benefit of light alloys.

OLD BRAIDS

FIGURE 75

Shows how two braids were made circa 1890. It is unlikely that this form of hairpin crochet had much real use. For the top braid the yarn is simply wound round the two prongs with the open end uppermost. Using a second yarn and starting at the rounded end of the pin a chain is worked over each loop up the centre, winding more yarn around the pin as required. The finished braid is unsatisfactory as the loops can be pulled through the central chains so that it easily becomes distorted. The lower braid shows three loops taken up with one chain.

Fig 74 An antique adjustable hairpin
Fig 75 An elementary method of hairpin crochet

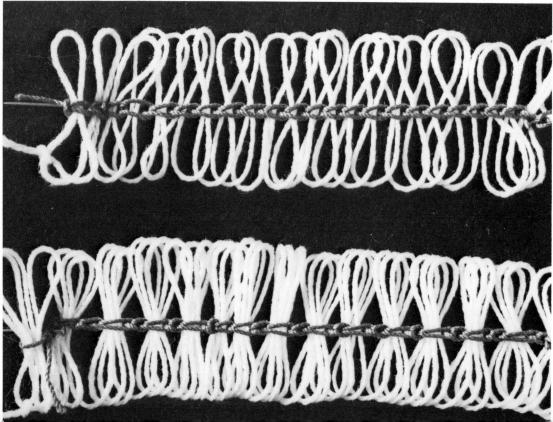

BIBLIOGRAPHY

BATH, Virginia Churchill, *Lace*, Studio Vista, 1974

DE DILLMONT, Theresa, *Encyclopaedia of Needlwork*, DMC Library, 1888

FELDMAN, Annette, *Handmade Lace and Patterns*, Harper and Row, 1978

GIFFORD, M.K., *Needlework*

GROVES, Silvia, *History of Needlework Tools and Accessories*, Country Life, 1966

KINMOND, Jean, *The Coats Book of Lacecrafts*, Batsford, 1978

KINMOND, Jean, *Crochet – Teach Yourself Books*, Hodder and Stoughton, 1979

KOSTER, Jane and MURRAY, Margaret, *New Crochet and Hairpin Work*, John Calder Pub. Ltd, 1955

NYE, Thelma, *The Batsford Book of Knitting and Crochet*, Batsford, 1973

STEARNS, Ann, *Batsford Book of Crochet*, Batsford, 1981

WALTERS, James, *Crochet Workshop*, Sidgwick and Jackson, 1979

WALTERS, James and COSH, Sylvia, *Crochet*, Octopus, 1980

WILLIAMS, Archibald (ed.), *The Hobby Books*, Thomas Nelson and Sons Ltd,

Every Woman's Encyclopaedia, c.1905

McCall's Needlework in Colour, Paul Hamlyn, 1964

Needlecraft, Vol. I, The Northern School of Needlework

Reader's Digest Complete Guide to Needlework, 1981

Weldon's Encyclopaedia of Needlework, Waverley Book Company, 1942

Young Ladies' Journal, 1874

SUPPLIERS

GREAT BRITAIN

Most needlework and wool shops stock
crochet hooks and yarns. Aero stockists may
supply hairpins.

These addresses have a mail order service
for the following:

CROCHET HOOKS, HAIRPINS, QUAD FRAMES AND
YARNS

The Handicraft Shop, Mail Order
Department, 47, Northgate, Canterbury,
Kent CT1 1BA. Telephone (0227) 69888.

FOR A WIDE RANGE OF CROCHET COTTONS AND
PERLE COTTONS

Spinning Jenny, Bradley, Keighley, West
Yorkshire. Telephone (0535) 32469.

RUG, CARPET AND CRAFT YARNS

Jackson's Rug Craft Ltd, Croft Mill, Hebden
Bridge, West Yorkshire.

Twilley's stockists can supply a wide range of
crochet and knitting cottons and lurex yarns.
For a list of stockists write to Twilleys,
Roman Mill, Stamford, Lincs. PE9 1SG.
Telephone Stamford 52661.

USA

For crochet hooks, hairpins and hairpin
looms – Hero stockists, who should be able
to order these items.

MAIL ORDER STOCKISTS FOR CROCHET SUPPLIES

American Handcrafts, 2617W Seventh Street,
Fort Worth, Texas 76707.

Economy Handicrafts, 50–21 69th Street,
Woodside, New York, N.Y. 113077.

Lee Ward, Elgin, Illinois 62120.

Peters Valley Craftsman, Layton, New Jersey
67851.

For a wide range of yarns including perle
cotton write for a list of stockists to:
Coats and Clarke Inc., 42 Park Avenue, New
York, N.Y.

INDEX

adhesive 26
antique
  braids 113
  doilies 74–81
  hairpins 115
  shawl 70
application 24
  borders 25
  edgings 24
  half edgings 25

bags
  Dorothy 40
  evening 88
  shopping 90
beads
  on borders 25
  on fringe 44
bed cape 84
belts
  appliqué motif 67
  lurex 45
  raffia 46
  wool 46
braid
  appliqué 21, 25, 40, 46, 67, 95
  basic 18, 21, 27–29, 30
  decorative 40, 45
  fan 34, 59, 60, 63, 74
  foundation 11, 30, 48
  lampshade 40, 44, 57

picot 33
stitchery on 25, 26, 67, 95, 98
working hints for 24

cable fabrics 53, 57
  heading 66
  joins 52
casting on 17, 104
coaster 73
collars 22, 37
corners
  joining 53
  turning a heading 37
  turning basic braid 25
crochet
  hook sizes 10, 11, 101
  lace 100
  stitches 11
curves 39, 41
curtains 44
cushions 40, 73, 86

decreasing 84
designing 102
doilies 72, 73–81, 113, 114–116
double twist 35

edgings 28–33, 104–109
  camisole 50
  chain lace 80

hairpin fabrics 55
handkerchiefs 13, 23, 28, 33, 37
household 23
round motifs 66
shell 33, 51, 66, 83, 109
towel 40
embroidery threads 24
equipment 14, 101, 115

fastening off 18
flounces 43
forks 14
frills
  handkerchief 42
  pram pillowcase 43
fringes 43
  bedspread 44
  jerkin 45
  knotted 56
  lampshades 44

hairpin
  braid laces 95, 98, 100
  fabrics 48, 54, 57, 58, 63, 86
  rounds 54, 64–70
  widths 11, 14, 101
hairpins 14, 15, 115
headings 32, 33, 36, 102
hooks 10, 11, 14, 101

improvised pins 15, 43
insertion patterns 32, 34
  evening bag 88
  sleeves 41
  suggestions 88

jackets 92
  blouson 94
  kimono 93
  long 94
joining methods 48
  cable 52
  chain lace 50
  chevron 49
  double crochet (sc) 49
  fans 60, 61
  picot 51
  shell 51
  using additional yarn 48,
    49
joining motifs 68

knitting cotton 23, 57

loops
  counting 24
  crossed 35
  double twist 35
  estimating 39, 103
  groups of 32

slip 16
  twisting 30

mohair 58, 70
motif centre crochet 64
motifs 64, 65, 67

perle cotton 23, 57
pillowcase border 40
place mats 57
poncho 84
pram blanket 55, 58
prongs 16

quadframe 15
  fringes 43
  to make 15

ribbon binding 55
  insertions 88
  threaded heading 36
rounds 64, 65, 69

sample making 39, 53, 102
scarves 58, 63
sequins 25, 67, 88
shawls
  Armenian 70, 71
  triangular 82
shopping bag 90

sleeve insertions 41
staples 14
string 57

table mats 57
  runners 57
treble (dc) heading 36

waistcoat 94
waste bins 40
window blind 44

yarns 14
  choice of 22, 102
  crochet cotton 28
  embroidery thread 24, 25
  estimating amounts 103
  knitting cotton 27
  lurex 24, 43, 102
  mohair 58
  novelty 24, 43, 102
  perle cotton 23, 57
  raffia type 46
  rayon cord 45
  rayon crochet 43, 57
  Russian braid 45
  sources of supply 101
  string 57, 102
  wool 23, 58
yoke appliqué 41, 67
  edging 41